Information Pathways

A Problem-Solving Approach to Information Literacy

CRYSTAL FULTON

THE SCARECROW PRESS, INC.
Lanham • Toronto • Plymouth, UK
2010

Published by Scarecrow Press, Inc.
A wholly owned subsidiary of The Rowman & Littlefield Publishing Group, Inc.
4501 Forbes Boulevard, Suite 200, Lanham, Maryland 20706
http://www.scarecrowpress.com

Estover Road, Plymouth PL6 7PY, United Kingdom

British Library Cataloguing in Publication Information Available

Library of Congress Cataloging-in-Publication Data

Fulton, Crystal, 1965–
  Information pathways : a problem-solving approach to information literacy /
Crystal Fulton.
    p. cm.
  Includes bibliographical references and index.
  ISBN 978-0-8108-7426-8 (pbk. : alk. paper) — ISBN 978-0-8108-7427-5 (ebook)
  1. Information literacy—Handbooks, manuals, etc. 2. Information retrieval—
Handbooks, manuals, etc. 3. Research—Methodology—Handbooks, manuals, etc.
4. Human information processing—Handbooks, manuals, etc. I. Title.
  ZA3075.F85 2010
  028.7—dc22
                                                                      2009047922

∞ ™ The paper used in this publication meets the minimum requirements of
American National Standard for Information Sciences—Permanence of Paper for
Printed Library Materials, ANSI/NISO Z39.48-1992.

Printed in the United States of America

For Julie and Nick—

The world of information is yours.

Contents

Acknowledgments

Writing this book has proven to be an incredible journey. I owe a great debt of thanks to so many people who have given their emotional support and input at different stages of this work.

This book never would have been possible without the love and support of my parents, Don and Marilyn. Thank you, Mom and Dad, for helping me to be the person I am and, most of all, for always believing that your daughter can do anything she wants to do.

My family, friends, and colleagues have been there for me throughout the writing process and have patiently listened to me go on endlessly about one part or another of this text. To Alan, my friends and work colleagues around the world, and a cast of thousands . . . Thanks for being there.

I am grateful for The Store, which served as my home away from home during much of the writing of this book. Sue, Will, Chris, and Joelle—you all make a fine latté. I'll always appreciate the stimulating conversations I enjoyed with the wonderful people I met in your café.

My editor, Martin Dillon, who showed unfailing patience while I wrote and edited chapters, has been a great mentor and friend.

And last, but certainly not least, I thank my students, who have been the inspiration for writing this book. Our work together helped me appreciate your ongoing journey through and relationship with an increasingly complex world in which mastery of information is central to your lives.

CHAPTER 1

Introduction: The Information Horizon

Imagine this: You are driving a vehicle along a major highway. As you drive along, you discover that the exit you require is closed. A very small sign is posted that indicates your options; however, the information presented is not only in a font so small it is barely readable from a distance but it also appears to be written in directional hieroglyphics. Faced with two exit options, which are now confusing to you, you randomly choose a pathway. You come across some minor roads that are clearly marked, but you do not recognize the names. Now you are lost. What information would critically help you make a decision right now in your journey? What would help you find your way again?

We all encounter situations in our daily lives in which a particular bit of information is vital to our decision making and progression along a path toward a future moment when we will feel we have solved the problem or question we wanted to answer. That information becomes the focus of our situation. The point is this: You need to be able to locate what you need when you need it, in a form that you can use immediately. Learning about pathways to information by understanding the different ways in which information is structured or not structured can help us make decisions to increase our chances of locating that proverbial needle in a haystack.

Who Will Benefit from Using This Book?

Information affects our lives in different ways at different times. This book is intended to help every reader improve his or her level of information literacy. In particular, the idea for this book emerged from my ongoing work with university students exploring the world of information around them and its importance to them not only in a university context but also in every aspect of their daily lives. As I worked with successive groups over the years, it became apparent that a textbook could really make a difference to students as they grappled with such concepts as bibliographic control within a continuously changing information landscape. Over and over again, students have asked me if there was one source that could answer all their questions about finding and using information. Although it is unlikely that this book will answer every question you might have, it is intended to equip you to take on information challenges on your own.

For the undergraduate or postgraduate student, this book supports learning about information problem solving in the classroom, potentially one where finding your way through information is the focus, or even part of the focus, of a given course. However, this text also provides a point of reference to which you can return for assistance whenever you feel uncertain or need to remind yourself of possible avenues to a particular type of information. As such, this book may be read in one sitting or dipped into when needed.

What This Book Will Do for You

This book will help you discover the ways in which information is structured, as well as not structured, to provide you with a breadcrumb trail to the answers you need or want to find. This book is not meant to answer specific information queries for you, and the sources discussed here do not form a comprehensive list by any means. There is a whole world of information beyond this book, but we can use some typical information situations to assist you in developing strategies you can then apply to similar information problems. For example, if you are hoping to discover a way to find information about a particular political dynasty, then you have come to the right book. However, this book will not identify the leaders of that political group for you.

Nil tam difficilest quin quaerendo invetigari possiet.
Nothing is so difficult but that it may be found out by seeking.

—Terence,
Heautontimoroumenos, iv, 2, 8

Importantly, you should take from this book the ability to solve an information problem. In the past, you may have tried remembering a few resources and applying them to every situation. You may believe, for instance, that an Internet search engine such as Google can answer every question you have. In reality, although this approach may produce results you value in part or as a whole, no search engine covers every one of the vast numbers of resources you might turn to in the course of a search for information. Problem solving is the key to successful and efficient information seeking. By thinking about the organization of information needed to answer a question and evaluating the information resources offering a potential answer, you will increase your level of information literacy and your confidence in your information problem-solving abilities, enabling you to function more effectively in your daily life.

> *Attempt the end, and never stand to doubt; nothing's so hard but search will find it out.*
>
> —Robert Herrick
> (1591–1674)

How This Book Is Organized

To enable you to develop your information problem-solving skills, this book is organized into chapters that examine different ways in which information is structured to help us navigate our way through it. Chapter 2 discuss the complexities of the information world around us and some of the concepts that are important to understanding this information world and considering information problems we encounter. Chapter 3 examines factual information, including direct and indirect means of accessing information. Chapter 4 focuses on navigating electronic information systems, including search query analysis, effective search strings, search evaluation, and sources such as the Internet and electronic databases that facilitate our electronic searching. Chapter 5 compares traditional means of organizing and accessing information through indexes, catalogues, and bibliographies with the more recent information systems that adopt a more fluid approach to the public's retrieval of information. Chapter 6 discusses formal and informal means of communicating information, including the publication process, communities of research, and overcoming problems associated with gray literature—that is, items over which there is no formal bibliographic control. Chapter 7 reviews the process of researching and writing. Chapter 8 offers strategies for strengthening our arguments by increasing our numeracy, our sophistication in using numbers. By functioning as informed citizens, we can take advantage of the immense world of numeric information published by governments.

Chapter 9 integrates the information skills we have learned throughout this text. We follow one particular group, genealogists, and explore how they have successfully mined information systems for information and circumvented established structures of information or used less well-known, specialized sources to build a complex knowledge base for themselves. We consider their strategies in bringing all our information skills to bear on retrieval problems in our own information worlds and consider means of overcoming possible barriers to meeting these challenges. Chapters 10 and 11 offer advice for maintaining the information literacy level you achieve as you progress through this textbook and for continuing to build on your successes with information.

Throughout this text, you will be given practical questions to test your learning. Take each information problem and extend it to a similar situation in your life in which you have needed information. Develop, evaluate, and re-evaluate your strategies for finding, evaluating, and adopting information. Return to specific chapters to revisit particular approaches to creating pathways to information. Remember, finding information can be an exciting adventure.

Now, let's get started.

CHAPTER 2

The Complex World of Information

We live in a world in which information holds paramount importance to navigating situations every day, yet wading into the world of information can be a complicated, overwhelming experience. Whether we need the latest weather forecast to plan a trip, step-by-step instructions for setting up a wireless computer network in our home, or a list of the side effects of combined drug therapies, information plays a vital role in our lives. We need information continuously and often quickly. This chapter examines what we know about information and the process of locating information.

What You Will Learn in This Chapter

In this chapter, we review what we know about information and the various aspects of our information behavior. By delving into these more theoretical issues, you will be able to do the following:

- Identify some key concepts, including information, information seeking, and information searching
- Relate aspects of how we approach information finding and use
- Develop personal goals for achieving information fluency
- Set up a blog diary to track your developing information literacy skills

Important Ideas and Terms to Consider as We Begin

WHAT IS INFORMATION?

Information is difficult to define, and it can mean many things to many people. It is relatively easy to think of information as words with value. For example, a sign posted in a window can provide us with valuable clues about an upcoming event or announcement. Associating information with text is second nature for us. However, we can find information in numerous other forms, including pictures, speech, and so forth.

So what do we mean by the term *information*? Information may include any textual, visual, or audio communication. In other words, information may be something we cannot even see. In addition, the word *information* is used as an all-encompassing term. It is important to separate information from data and knowledge and to understand the continuum of these terms.

DATA

The term *data* usually refers to unprocessed information, what we might think of as information in the raw. Data occur as audio, text, numbers, pictures, and so on that are, on their own, without meaning provided by context. Consider several numbers or words listed on a piece of paper. Each item stands alone, without particular meaning or relationships.

INFORMATION

Data become information when a grouping or structure is imposed on the data items. For example, several words, such as *horrific, saccharine, superior, twisted,* and *watchable,* have no particular context. However, if we couple these words with movie titles, then suddenly, these words become succinct reviews of particular movies. The data now have context, convey meaning, and may be called information.

KNOWLEDGE

Knowledge refers to understanding gained from imposing structure and creating meaning from data and/or information. We do this instinctively, collecting bits of data and information and making sense of what we now have in the context of our world. By relying on our experience and understanding of this context, we can then make decisions about what does and does not belong in a particular grouping of data and information.

Working with Data, Information, and Knowledge

Data, information, and knowledge may be collected and stored in information resources. An information resource is a tool that contains facts or other data, information, and knowledge of possible relevance to a question we might have. Although the terms *source* and *resource* are often used interchangeably, they do technically differ. A source refers to the origin or beginning point of something—for example, the initiation of a flu pandemic or fashion trend, or the starting point of a river. A resource, on the other hand, offers a supply of material that may help to solve a problem. Resources can range from collected information tools, such as the Internet Movie Database, www.imdb.com, to whole libraries.

> *Knowledge is of two kinds. We know a subject ourselves, or we know where we can find information upon it.*
>
> —Samuel Johnson

Information Behavior, Information Seeking, and Information Searching

Information behavior, information seeking, and *information searching* are interrelated terms. Wilson (1999) demonstrates the relationships among the three terms in his nested model of information behavior (see figure 2.1).

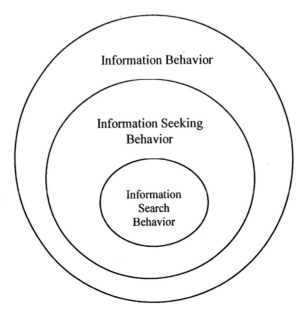

Figure 2.1.   Wilson's (1999) Nested Model of Information Behavior

Information behavior or IB refers to the wider arena of our combined cognitive and affective responses as we engage with information. Information behavior is a holistic term, encompassing those activities surrounding our interaction with information worlds around us. This includes all activities we associate with information, such as looking for information, accessing information, and using information.

Another key phrase for our journey through information is *information-seeking behavior* or ISB. As Wilson's diagram illustrates, our information-seeking behavior reflects only part of our overall information behavior. Information seeking is a subset of information-behavior activities and is focused on how we develop pathways to information to satisfy an information goal or challenge. *Information searching* is a further subset of information seeking. Our work together in this text not only concerns information activities that fall within information searching, including our interactions with information retrieval systems as we look for information, but also extends to related information activities, such as evaluation and management of information.

Quick Tips: Identifying and Analyzing an Information Need or Want

Understanding that you must solve an information problem and identifying the nature of that problem are critical for planning a way forward through information.
Ask yourself:

- What is my information problem? What, if anything, needs solving?
- What are the different aspects of this problem?
- What information would resolve this problem?

These concepts associated with information behavior apply to the range of reasons we might have for interacting with information and information resources, often generally categorized as our *information needs* and *information wants*. Although we might mix the terms *need* and *want* in conversation, it is important to distinguish between the two and their potential effect on our motivation and action to locate information. An information need refers to information we must have in order to progress with an activity. For example, to process a work visa to work abroad, you must, at some point, provide government officials in that country with your passport as proof of identity. Producing your passport, as well as knowing how to obtain a current passport, form immediate needs in this instance. You cannot move forward in processing your work visa without this documentation.

Want refers to desire. A piece of information might enhance a particular information situation, but it is not essential to resolving an information problem. For example, we may want all of our information to be available through a particular resource or in a particular format, but we do not necessarily need for this to be the case. If we consider an everyday life situation, we may want to eat dessert—but it is not generally something we would consider a dietary need.

HOW OUR EMOTIONS INFLUENCE OUR INFORMATION BEHAVIOR

Our emotions accompany us and guide our information behavior. Many researchers, such as Nahl (2007), continue to explore the role of emotions in determining our responses to information problems in different areas of our lives. Our emotional responses occur alongside our cognitive responses to situations; we feel and we think as we make decisions about how to explore, accept, and manage information.

We experience a range of emotions as we interact with information. For example, we may feel elated at locating that last nugget of information to complete a report. However, we can also experience frustration and anxiety with information seeking, for example, when we are unsure of where to begin, what sources to consult, or whether an answer to our question actually exists. How many times have you felt happy, frustrated, excited, or pessimistic about finding and using information?

> *Feeling without judgement is a washy draught indeed; but judgement untempered by feeling is too bitter and husky a morsel for human deglutition.*
>
> *—Charlotte Brontë, Jane Eyre*

You might argue that the Internet has changed the information landscape to provide information instantly and everywhere. The Internet does provide quick and easy access to a wide array of information, but have you ever felt overwhelmed at the same time by the thousands and even millions of items retrieved in an Internet search? Internet searchers are more likely to find too much information, as opposed to too little, and then possibly not the information best suited to resolving their information problem.

As a result, feelings of becoming stressed, overwhelmed, and lost in cyberspace are not uncommon. This phenomenon is variously labeled *information anxiety, information overload,* or *data smog.* Shenk (1997) first referred to this problem as data smog, declaring that an overabundance of information can reduce our effectiveness in finding and using information in our everyday lives.

As Shenk (2007) notes, "In our work, home, and social lives, we are saturated with data and stimulus. While our grandparents were limited by access to information and speed of communication, we are restricted largely by our ability to wade through it all." Shenk's work reminds us that it is important to

> *Information networks straddle the world. Nothing remains concealed. But the sheer volume of information dissolves the information. We are unable to take it all in.*
>
> *—Günther Grass (1927–), Interview in New Statesman & Society, June 22, 1990*

consider our positive and negative emotional responses to information situations. Learning to locate, evaluate, utilize, and manage information effectively and efficiently can help us reduce those feelings of overloading and help us to assert control over information.

INFORMATION-SEARCHING ACTIVITIES

When we search for information, we engage in multiple activities. Particular aspects of the act of seeking attend our behavior, including querying, searching, and browsing.

Querying

Querying refers to asking questions or making inquiries about a particular thing. This part of information seeking involves an explicit task as well as evaluation. For example, you might be asked, "What is your search query?" In this case, this is the question that forms the basis of your search for a particular source.

Searching

Searching involves exploring something to locate information. It is characterized by thorough examination, which distinguishes searching from querying. For example, you might wish to find information about a given subject—growing hothouse tomatoes for fun and profit, for example. You might search several databases for information.

Browsing

Browsing is a more casual and less-targeted activity than either querying or searching. Although querying and searching rely on navigating set system paths, browsing allows greater flexibility. The individual browsing may still navigate pathways formulated by another, such as hyperlinks on a web page; however, the individual has greater choice among pathways.

For example, the traditional organization of information in a book is a beginning, middle, and conclusion, with discrete chapters, prefacing materials such as a table of contents, and so forth, routinely anticipated. Although a reader can be expected to read a book from beginning to end, you might elect to read the ending first or start at another part of the book, reading small sections randomly or as they interest you. Some would say that you were spoiling a story by deviating from the traditional linear notion of reading; however, others might say you were merely altering your reading experience by exploring the material presented from a different viewpoint.

Information Activities and Information Literacy

Although the activities outlined above are specific to our information searching, our overall information behavior includes additional information activities, such as evaluating, collecting, organizing, managing, and presenting information. These additional aspects of our information behavior are key features of the information-literate individual and life-long learner. Becoming information literate involves the mastery of these information activities. As Bruce (2003) suggests, being information literate involves "the ability to access, evaluate, organise and use information in order to learn, problem-solve, make decisions in formal and informal learning contexts, at work, at home and in educational settings."

Stern's (2002) report for UNESCO highlights improving all forms of literacy as a means of combating poverty. UNESCO defines five forms of literacy:

1. Alphabetic literacy, which, in its most basic form, refers to a person being able to write his or her own name.
2. Functional reading and writing literacy, which allows a person to read or write on the most elementary and basic levels of everyday life.
3. Social literacy, which empowers one to read, write, and communicate effectively using the cultural language of a particular community (e.g., awareness of linguistic social norms and practices, language dialects, body language as communication, and unspoken communication customs).

4. Information literacy, which requires people to use critical thinking skills to "locate, evaluate, and use information in order to become independent learners" (www.ala.org/acrl/ilcomstan.html).

5. Digital information literacy, which refers to a person's ability to use information literacy skills in electronic environments such as the Internet or digital databases. Included in digital information literacy are emerging literacies such as computer, network, software, visual, multimedia, audio, tool, and Internet literacy (Stern 2002).

The Association of Colleges and Research Libraries (ACRL) (2000) division of the American Libraries Association (ALA) has set forth five standards for information literacy, each of which has specific objectives:

1. *Know:* The information-literate student determines the nature and extent of the information needed.

2. *Access:* The information-literate student accesses needed information effectively and efficiently.

3. *Evaluate:* The information-literate student evaluates information and its sources critically and incorporates selected information into his or her knowledge base and value system.

4. *Use:* The information-literate student, individually or as a member of a group, uses information effectively to accomplish a specific purpose.

5. *Ethical/Legal:* The information-literate student understands many of the economic, legal, and social issues surrounding the use of information and accesses and uses information ethically and legally.

The Council of Australian University Librarians (CAUL) (2001) has modified the ACRL's list to include two additional standards:

1. *Control/Manipulate:* The information-literate person classifies, stores, manipulates, and redrafts information collected or generated.

2. *Information Literacy for Lifelong Learning:* The information-literate person recognizes that lifelong learning and participative citizenship require information literacy.

Information literacy is a long-term goal throughout the world. However, remember that you can help yourself as well by working toward a deeper understanding of your own patterns of information behavior, including your evaluation and use of information you find.

Educators, librarians, and concerned individuals have promoted learning information literacy for some time now. However, you also have a role to play. Consider what you can do to help yourself develop and maintain your own information literacy.

Monitoring Our Progress

As we begin building pathways through information, we will want to monitor our progress. Recording our experiences with information as we go along will enable us to reflect upon what and how we are learning about information. One way to observe our ongoing development of information problem-solving skills is to keep a diary detailing our information activities. A blog is a form of online diary that offers us an easy means of tracking our experiences. Writing about information problems encountered and resolved, and then reflecting upon this process documented in our diary entries over time, can help us identify patterns in our responses to information situations and means of overcoming obstacles.

Outlined below are instructions for starting a blog to keep as you work through this text. We'll check in with

> My Blog:
>
> *is a place where I think, plan and reflect*
> *forces me to read in order to gather the input I need for my output*
> *is a place where I play with technology and ideas*
> *often surprises me*
> *is a place where I collaborate*
> *is currently the most satisfying part of my job*
> *is slightly dangerous*
> *is compulsive*
>
> —www.microbiologybytes .com/AJC/whyblog.html

our blogs to see how we are progressing with our journey through information. In the meantime, start writing in your blog often and in detail. Document not only your information successes but also the barriers that hamper your efforts to resolve information problems. Reflect periodically on your work and consider alternative approaches to information challenges.

These instructions will help you start your own blog to record your experiences with information. The skills you learn will also help you participate in future blogging.

—ɯ—

Exercise 1: Creating a Personal Blog Using Google's Blogger.com

I. Getting Started
   A. Go to www.blogger.com.
   You will be asked to log in using your Gmail account.
      1. If you have a Gmail account, then log in using your Gmail username and password, or
      2. If you do not have a Gmail account, you will need to create an account. Select *Create Your Blog Now* and fill in the online form that appears.
   B. Select *Create a blog* and follow the online instructions to name your blog and choose a URL for your blog. *Important!* Be sure to record all access information, including your Gmail account, title of your blog, and URL for your blog in a secure place for future reference.
   C. Choose one of the color and layout templates provided in Blogger.com to format your blog.

II. Customizing Your Blog. Once you have created your blog, you should customize your blog to enable or disable access by others, according to your personal preference.
   A. Customizing Privacy Settings
      1. Select *Customize*.
      2. Select *Settings* tab. You should by default see the screen menu for the *Basic* settings tab.
      3. Select *Yes* or *No* in response to *Add your blog to our listings?* according to your personal preference for public viewing access to your blog.
      4. Select *Yes* or *No* in response to *Show email post links?* according to your personal preference for public viewing access to your blog.
   B. Inviting Others to Participate
      1. Select the *Permissions* tab.
      2. Under Blog Authors, select *Add Authors*.
      3. In the *Invite more people to write to your blog* box, type the e-mail address of a person you wish to invite to participate in your blog.

    4. Select *Invite*. An invitation will be e-mailed to this person. Once he or she has accepted your invitation, you will be able to see that person's name listed under the heading *Contributors* on your blog.

    5. Under *Blog Readers—Who can read this blog?* select *Only blog authors*, if you wish to limit participation to particular individuals.

    6. Then confirm this action by selecting *Allow authors only* from the pop-up window. You can eliminate Steps 5 and 6 if you wish to allow full public access to your blog.

C. Adding Comments to Your Blog

    1. Select *New Post*. An empty box will appear.

    2. Type your comments.

    3. Select *Publish Post*.

    4. Select *View Blog* to see your post as published on your blog.

Exercise 2: Dear Blog . . .

What are your personal goals for improving your information literacy? Writing in your blog, describe your information world, including information challenges you face every day and sources you use frequently. If there is a picture, cartoon, or drawing that sums up your current information world, then add this to your blog.

    Now explain what you would like to change about your relationship with information. Set three goals for yourself to accomplish as you progress through this textbook.

CHAPTER 3

Finding Factual Information

We need factual information on an ongoing basis in our daily lives. In fact, every day we are inundated by bits of factual information that we may opt to use to help us solve an information problem. By factual information, we mean information that may be verified as correct or incorrect. This type of information may take a range of forms, from numerical information to a short entry in a source about a particular topic. Consider some of the factual information that is at your fingertips. Something as simple as today's weather forecast provides a wealth of information: expected temperatures for the day, anticipated precipitation or sunshine, projected weather conditions for the next few days, comparative weather conditions past and present, and so on.

In this chapter, we explore ways of solving information problems with factual information, keeping in mind some of the typical published sources and publication formats to facilitate finding this kind of information. As always, the key to success in locating factual information is to understand the nature of the problem you wish to solve and the organization of the information relevant to solving this problem.

What You Will Learn in This Chapter

In this chapter, we focus on factual information. By considering the nature of factual information and the array of sources that provide this type of information, you will learn to do the following:

• Understand what is meant by a fact-finding or reference tool
• Consider some of the resources that facilitate fact finding
• Appreciate the organization of factual information
• Explore the role of this type of information in our everyday lives

Tools That Facilitate Access to Factual Information

As you search for factual information, you are likely to use a particular formal channel of information known as a reference tool for information. As the word *reference* implies, this tool refers us to information and other sources of information. Reference resources are designed to help you find a particular piece of information without having to read the entire publication.

In libraries, reference tools are generally housed in one area near an information desk. Although you may consult this type of material in the library, in general, you would not be able to borrow this material as you would materials from other library collections. A reference collection may include materials in a variety of formats, including books, CD-ROMs, and so forth. Similar reference tools appear on the Internet. Collections of reference resources—for example, the Internet Public Library, www.ipl.org—are useful ways of identifying new and sometimes evaluated sources of information. Regardless of format, the function of the tool remains the same.

Pathways to Information through Standard Reference Resources

We can divide reference resources into two categories, according to their role in our information seeking: direct access and indirect access. While catalogues, bibliographies, and indexes, as discussed in chapter 5, provide citations or pointers to information sources, other reference resources provide information at a glance. Direct information resources, such as encyclopedias, usually provide factual information about an event or person or place. Various resources provide specialized information; for instance, an atlas focuses on geographical information.

You will find that different sorts of reference tools can be used to locate similar information. In addition, some tools will appear mislabeled in their titles; for example, the *Encyclopedia of World Biography* may seem oddly titled, mixing the terms *encyclopedia* and *biography* in one tool, but consider the ways in which tools with dual designations satisfy multiple classifications. Reference tools provide factual information, regardless of title. It is also useful to consider the general characteristics of the main, direct reference tools, then apply this information to selecting the appropriate type of tool to resolve particular information problems.

Identifying the Proper Tool to Solve a Given Information Query

HANDBOOKS

A good starting point for your search is often a handbook. A handbook, also called a manual, is a type of reference tool that provides factual information about a particular subject, such as traditions for celebrating holidays and anniversaries, or instructions to complete a task. For example, *The Cloud Collector's Handbook* (2009) provides quick reference facts about clouds to help cloud-spotters identify particular cloud formations. *The Study Skills Handbook* (2008) offers tips for developing positive study habits. The *Guinness Book of World Records* contains factual nuggets about record breaking around the world. As instructional manuals, handbooks may also provide such information as the rules for playing a particular sport. For instance, consider a recipe book, such as *Nosh 4 Students: A Fun Student Cookbook* (2006), which explains how to make particular culinary dishes. A book of recipes is really a handbook or instruction manual for cooking. A single handbook can also fulfill multiple functions; the *Chicago Manual of Style*, for example, not only provides guidance in writing skills and bibliographic citations but may also be used to answer questions such as "Where would I find a list of proofreader's marks?" or "What does the Latin term *ibid* mean and when should I use it?"

Handbooks can be especially helpful in the beginning stages of a search for information by serving as a pointing device to potential sources of information in a given subject area. For instance, *Walford's Guide to Reference Material* is a standard reference tool that can help orient you to particular bodies of reference tools. *Walford's* is split into multiple volumes, divided by general subject areas, with separate indexes for each volume. If we wanted to locate information about a current or retrospective newsworthy item, we would select the appropriate volume and locate the subject heading *newspapers*, under which we will find an array of newspaper titles from different countries, accompanied by short descriptions of each, coverage, publication frequency, and so on. In short, we are provided with a set of factual information about each newspaper listed. Although the list provided is unlikely to be comprehensive, we are still able to gain insight into the type of source we wish to examine, as well as some of the main titles of newspapers potentially of interest in our search. A guide like *Walford's* should be considered when you are unsure where to start your search or of the sorts of information tools that might assist you in your search. For the most comprehensive approach to a search, use this type of guide as a starting point and expand your search to guides that are focused solely on a given subject.

Just as a number of handbooks are available in printed format, a proliferation of handbooks in the style of "how-to" guides also exists on the Internet. For example, Berkeley Library's long-standing guide *Finding Information on the Internet*, available at www.lib.berkeley.edu/TeachingLib/Guides/Internet/FindInfo.html, offers tutorials and handouts for learning how to search for information on the Internet. Discovery Communications' *How Stuff Works*, www.howstuffworks.com, explains phenomena queried by the general public.

Although these guides may be deemed reliable because of their creators, other similar online resources are produced by the trend toward online, collective public knowledge generation. For instance, a quick search of YouTube, www.youtube.com, will locate numerous video clips posted by members of the public about a wide variety of topics. *Videojug: Life Explained on Film*, www.videojug.com, is a well-known member of the online genre of how-to guides, in this case one of the many projects where anyone can contribute to building a collection of instructional videos, some serious and some less so, without restrictions on the nature of content.

ALMANACS

An almanac is a collected work of factual information about a particular year. Almanacs characteristically include political, historical, and current events, as well as calendar and astronomical information. For instance, an almanac might feature the top news stories of a particular year, a chronology of the past year's events, and lists of people who distinguished themselves in particular ways during the year. In addition to textually displayed facts, almanacs may present statistical information and illustrations. When searching for information in an almanac, be sure to remember that they are usually published annually and therefore provide information for the year prior to publication. As with other reference tools, almanacs may be subject focused, such as the *International Television and Video Almanac* and the *Texas Almanac*, www.texasalmanac.com, or more general in content, such as the *World Almanac and Book of Facts* and the *World Almanac for Kids*, www.worldalmanacforkids.com.

A familiar example of an almanac is the *Farmer's Almanac*, published in North America since 1792 in print form and more recently online as well at www.almanac.com. As is typical of almanacs, the *Farmer's Almanac* offers information ranging from recipes to weather predictions and astronomical information, including sunrise and sunset, moon phases, and seasonal information. In addition, the *Farmer's Almanac* contains useful tips, for example, for gardening and outdoor activities. An almanac such as this one may be used to answer questions like "What firewood has the best heat value?" "What should be packed in an emergency car kit?" and "How do you tie knots?" In addition, this almanac provides historical information, including past weather information and events that took place on a given day in history.

> *Time to plant tears, says the almanac.*
>
> —Elizabeth Bishop

BIOGRAPHICAL RESOURCES

As the name implies, biographical resources provide factual information about people. You may be familiar with biographies, which offer the story of an individual's life, and autobiographies, which are life stories written by the individuals themselves. A biographical resource, such as the *Dictionary of Egyptian Gods and Goddesses* or the *Dictionary of Culprits and Criminals*, provides short biographical sketches about individuals relevant to a particular subject area.

Collections of obituaries are another common form of biographical resource; for example, www.legacy.com's collection of obituaries published in papers worldwide, or the well-known *New York Times*' obituaries, www.nytimes.com. Biographical information is intended to be factual, covering the significant aspects of a person's life history. Entries are generally indexed alphabetically by surnames.

> *Biography is a system in which the contradictions of a human life are unified.*
>
> —José Ortega y Gasset

The *Who's Who* is a well-established biographical resource, including a broad range of Who's Who publications. Among these are the *International Who's Who*, *Who's Who in the World*, *Who's Who in Medicine and Healthcare*, and *Who's Who of Victorian Cinema*, not to mention the various *Who Was Who* publications, which provide retrospective biographical information. In fact, the number of *Who's Who* titles is so extensive that one can nearly imagine any Who's Who title and then find that a volume on the topic has been published.

You may wonder why biographical resources differ in their coverage of people. Although two biographical resources may cover similar topics, their inclusion of individuals may differ greatly. Inclusion in a biographical resource may be highly selective and may be a source of bias in the tool, particularly since people sometimes pay a fee to be included in a given resource. It is essential to remain vigilant in your evaluation of the information you find in a biographical resource, keeping in mind that you may be reading what an individual would like known about himself or herself, as opposed to a full account of that person's life.

One attempt to circumvent the subscription approach to inclusion may be found in *Who's Who Online*, www.whoswho-online.com. Although this site offers biographical information as submitted by individuals themselves to document their online accomplishments, there is no charge for membership or for public access to the biographical sketches selected for publication from those submitted.

DICTIONARIES

We usually think of dictionaries as factual reference works that provide definitions for words or specific terminology, pronunciation, grammar, usage in language, and the etymological history of a given word. *The Oxford English Dictionary* is an example of a well-known dictionary tool that serves these functions. Dictionaries may also be focused on one aspect of language. For example, *A Dictionary of Cantonese Slang: The Language of Hong Kong Movies, Street Gangs and City Life* and the *Urban Dictionary*, www.urbandictionary.com, provide definitions and explanations of the vernacular usage of language in particular contexts. Online versions of slang dictionaries may offer the option to add terms, making them organic dictionaries that evolve with language.

> *Impossible is a word to be found only in the dictionary of fools.*
>
> —Napoleon Bonaparte

All of these dictionaries have in common an alphabetical arrangement of words that facilitates easy access of the word about which information is required. Of course, electronic dictionaries also provide search mechanisms that enable the searcher to locate words without following the alphabetical sequence of a printed dictionary. *Dictionary.com*, www.dictionary.com, also offers searching of one or many dictionary tools, including dictionaries for translating between languages, crossword dictionaries, specialized legal and medical dictionaries, as well as links to thesauri and other types of reference tools noted in this chapter.

A different type of dictionary tool is a dictionary of quotations. This form of dictionary is very helpful in identifying the person who said a particular phrase, the wording of famous phrases, and the evolution of a phrase over time through various personalities who have varied the original phrase. One of the most famous dictionaries of quotations is *Bartlett's Familiar Quotations*, www.bartleby.com. In its online version, it is expanded to offer searching of a collection of dictionaries of quotations, other dictionaries, thesauri, and similar resources. Dictionaries of quotations may also be helpful when used in conjunction with other subject sources. For example, if you were studying Shakespeare's plays and poetry, you would require the full text of his works; however, you could easily access particular passages through a *Dictionary of Quotations from Shakespeare*, which identifies speakers and plays associated with these passages.

DIRECTORIES

A directory is generally a list of people or organizations, including information such as names of people and the office or position held, affiliations, addresses, telephone numbers, and web addresses. Arrangement may be alphabetic by name or subject area.

The directory we are all probably most familiar with is our local telephone directory. Also commonly known as the "white pages," telephone directories may vary slightly in arrangement, with some separating residential entries from business numbers; however, the overall format is generally the same. Telephone directories provide access to name, telephone number, and address information for people and organizations for a given area. Keep in mind that only those individuals and businesses who agree to have their contact information included in the directory will be found there; an individual or business may also elect not to have such information published. The *Yellow* or *Golden Pages*, entitled according to different regions but generally printed on yellow paper, provides alternative access to business information. Organizations appear in alphabetical order, classed by type of organization or service.

Telephone directories are usually circulated free of charge, although some organizations charge for information acquired via their Internet websites. In recent years, many telephone companies have made their annual directories available electronically as well as in standard print format. Internet access to telephone directories has enabled more means of searching, including reverse lookup functions. For instance, the *Reverse Phone Directory*, www.reversephonedirectory.com, provides searching of white pages, directory assistance or 411 directories, and toll-free numbers in North America by telephone number and address, rather than by name alone. *WhitePages.com*, www.whitepages.com, also offers a reverse lookup function, as well as searching of toll-free numbers (including toll-free numbers that contain alpha and numeric telephone numbers), registered telephone numbers, and international telephone directories. The proliferation of publicly available telephone directories has encouraged the development of directories of telephone directories with full online search capabilities. For

example, a Belgium company, Kapitol, initiated *Infobel* at www.infobel
.com/teldir, a free directory service that also provides access to telephone
directories worldwide.

In addition to telephone directories, other directories may also list a
variety of information. For instance, trade directories list contact information for manufacturers, wholesalers, and suppliers by industry. The
directory may be country specific as well as trade specific. In addition, the
information may be used retrospectively; for example, *Pigot's Trade Directories*, which date back to the nineteenth century, may be used to trace a
person or business over time.

Individual organizations and associations may similarly publish specific information relevant to locating members and their function within
the organization or association, identifying the varying functions of the
group and providing access to information about the group via the Internet. Organizations may also publish subject-oriented directories, which
guide the user to information about institutions, services, and individuals. Peterson's directories are well-established publications in the field of
education. Collectively presented on the Internet at www.petersons.com,
these educational directories maintain information about North American
educational institutions, crossing all educational levels and subject areas
for different groups of students, including international students and
postgraduate students.

Although a number of established directories and lists of directories
exist in both print and electronic formats, new and evolving technologies
and uses of technologies that feature in Web 2.0 present new challenges to
finding information in list form. As information content is created, there
is commonly a parallel movement to try and organize that information in
some fashion. The difficulty lies in trying to keep up, and some authors
(e.g., Weinberger, 2007) even argue that organization is irrelevant and
impossible, and instead we should focus on the power of messiness or
miscellany in digital information.

ENCYCLOPEDIAS

Encyclopedias offer convenient access to summaries of factual information
that may help us in our daily lives, as well as in our academic studies. Use
an encyclopedia when you need to find facts about a variety of topics,

Transient Information: Tools for Organizing and Locating Blogs

Locating blogs offers a typical challenge in this sort of quickly evolving and transient information. Blogs have captured many people's imagination, with estimates of millions of blogs in existence and more blogs coming online daily. Although this area of information is rapidly changing, various attempts have been made to improve access to blogs. Access can prove particularly important for those whose blogs have a strong following.

Developing lists of blogs—really, the directory format—for locating blogs lends itself naturally to the web. Blog lists appear in several venues online, and lists of top blogs are popular. For example, the *Guardian* newspaper offers a list of what might be considered fifty of the world's most influential blogs, www.guardian.co.uk/technology/2008/mar/09/blogs. *Blog Storm*, www.blogstorm.co.uk/top-100-uk-blogs, ranks a Top 100 list of United Kingdom blogs, while *Technorati*, http://technorati.com/pop/blogs, provides a Top 100 ranking of blogs across the Internet. Word Press, http://wordpress.com, not only provides rankings of the top blogs using Word Press's blogging software but also ranks popular posts and growing blogs. *Blogs on Top*, aka BOT, www.blogsontop.com, enables bloggers to submit their blogs to its list, then categorizes blogs by subject and tracks the popularity of blogs over time.

Other blog directories focus on gathering blogs, sometimes on a specific topic. For example, claiming to be the web's oldest blog directory, *Eaton Web: The Blog Directory* collects blogs on a variety of topics, organizes the blogs into categories, and assesses blog growth or decline. *Blog Catalog*, www.blogcatalog.com, refers to itself as a social community for bloggers and one of the largest blog directories on the Internet. Blogs are located in categories arranged as folders under the heading "Directory," and search functions enable searching blogs. A Discussion area provides a Twitter-like function, where bloggers can discuss any topic, and a Groups area enables social networking groups around particular topics. The *Internet Public Library's Blog List*, www.ipl.org/div/blogs, includes lists of blogs as well as advice for creating and searching blogs.

Search engines dedicated to finding blogs are also useful, particularly since blogs come and go rapidly. Google offers Blog Search, http://blog-search.google.com, which enables searching the Internet blogosphere by keyword or through precategorized areas. In addition, just as you can set up a notification of the posting of new materials on a given topic in many electronic systems, Google's Blog Search provides options to create e-mail alerts and subscribe to blog feeds in Google Reader, as well as linking a particular blog to your Google homepage. Similarly, other blog search engines offer search facilities for tracking blogs through the Internet, such as *Blog Search Engine* at www.blogsearchengine.com. Remember, blog search engines depend upon constant acquisition and evaluation of content, so if you cannot locate your blog using a blog search engine, then ask yourself:

- Have you submitted your blog to the blog search engine site for inclusion?
- Have you updated your blog recently to maximize continuing interest in your blog?
- Have you considered alternative search terms?

To locate a list of blog search engines, try *Ask.com*'s *Blog Search Engine* list, http://websearch.about.com/od/internetresearch/a/newsblog.htm, and see which blog search engine works best for you.

including events, people, and places. For students, encyclopedias are useful as a pre-search tool. For instance, you might consult an encyclopedia for general background information about a topic that is unfamiliar to you. This approach is a particularly useful strategy in the beginning stages of essay writing, discussed further in chapter 7 of this textbook.

The actual content of an encyclopedia consists of generally short articles that provide factual information about a topic. However, pictures, diagrams, and other visual content may accompany text; encyclopedias found online offer an even wider array of content, including multimedia features such as video and sound. Content may target particular audiences. For instance, Oxford's *Children's Encyclopedia*, published as a CD-ROM, provides multimedia information geared toward the linguistic and comprehension levels of primary school children. An encyclopedia may also

> A man is the whole encyclopedia of facts.
>
> —Ralph Waldo Emerson

be subject specific, providing an array of factual information covering all aspects of a topic, often in a more in-depth fashion than is possible in a general encyclopedia. For example, a subject-specific encyclopedia, such as the *Great Soviet Encyclopedia*, an English translation of the original Russian version, offers coverage of topics related to that particular country that the publisher notes are not necessarily covered in depth in other English-language sources.

In printed format, encyclopedias may be published in one or multiple volumes. For instance, one famous encyclopedia, the *Encyclopedia Britannica*, has traditionally appeared in a series of volumes, now replaced by the online version of this tool at www.britannica.com. The online version offers a relatively simple means of updating information, whereas previously new information was added to the encyclopedia set by publishing supplements and yearbooks on an annual basis. Arrangement of information within an encyclopedia is alphabetical by topic.

The growth of user-generated content has helped change the appearance and expand the traditional content of encyclopedias. The best-known online encyclopedia created and edited by the public is probably Wikipedia, www .wikipedia.com. Known for its use of collaborative wiki technology, Wikipedia allows anyone to publish content at its site. This openness has left the encyclopedia exposed to the posting of false information. Although, in theory, the public's collaborative posting and editing of information is intended to improve quality and reliability of content, verification of information found via Wikipedia is generally considered important. In spite of potential issues with quality of information, Wikipedia is now widely used, and it offers a serious contender to the long-standing Encyclopedia Britannica, which has developed such features as a blog to attract readership.

> Wikipedia is the best thing ever. Anyone in the world can write anything they want about any subject. So you know you are getting the best possible information.
>
> —Michael Scott, *The Office*, "The Negotiation" (Season 3, Episode 18, 2007)

GEOGRAPHICAL RESOURCES

Geographical resources are most often used to answer questions concerning location or space. At some point, it is likely that you have consulted a geographical resource to locate a place. For instance, you may have used a map of a certain city to find a route from one point to another in that city. Common names for geographical resources reflect the different types of geographical resources; for instance, the *National Geographic Atlas of the World* and Oxford University's *Atlas of the World* both suggest that you will find in them location information for the entire planet Earth.

Quick Tips: Britannica v. Wikipedia: How Can Each Satisfy Your Information Problem?

BRITANNICA

- Content created by subject experts
- Public can suggest content modifications to Britannica editors, who edit content
- Content partially available freely; full content available by subscription
- Audio and pictorial content included
- References provided alongside content
- Hyperlinks provided to outside content
- Google widget available

WIKIPEDIA

- Content collaboratively created by the public, although some have argued that many subject experts actually contribute strongly to content
- Content can be edited by the public
- Content freely viewable
- Audio and pictorial content included
- References may or may not be provided
- Hyperlinks provided to outside content
- Google widget available

Other resources have unique names and provide unique functions; for example, a gazetteer lists geographical names or physical features of an area, sometimes profiling communities. This type of resource is very useful for gathering retrospective, historical information about a community. While a map or atlas may provide a two-dimensional device for locating places, a globe provides similar information on a larger, worldview scale. Depending on the geographical resource, levels of detail vary from pinpointing minute locations to satellite snapshots from much farther away.

The key to understanding a geographical resource, such as a map or atlas, is a grid system of invisible lines around Earth called longitude and latitude. Longitude refers to the vertical, equidistant lines that run from pole to pole. Latitude denotes the equidistant lines running horizontally around the planet, measured in degrees northwards and southwards from the equator. We use the intersection of lines of latitude and longitude to locate places. For example, you might have a globe on your desk that shows lines of latitude and longitude. Atlases not only map different regions but also generally provide an index of named places and their associated degrees of longitude and latitude that refer us then to particular points within the atlas's maps.

The Internet and GPS (Global Positioning System) have changed the way in which many users access and understand geographical resources. The Internet has enabled users to access electronic geographical tools with mapping capabilities beyond those of printed maps. A much-used electronic mapping service is MapQuest, www.mapquest.com and www.map quest.co.uk, which provides one-stop shopping for a variety of geographic information, such as a world atlas and quick facts about countries, including official languages, flags, capital cities, life expectancy, government type, currency, population, size, and industry. Google Maps, http://maps .google.com, similarly provides a world map you can move like a globe, but this time zooming into locations to street level, enabling virtual strolls in neighborhoods with a unique Street View function. Street View further connects the viewer to additional content, such as photographs taken in a particular area by contributing members of the public. A powerful aspect of both MapQuest and Google Maps is their mapping feature that helps the viewer chart a course from Point A to Point B, even providing stepwise driving and walking instructions that can then be printed, e-mailed, or downloaded to a handheld electronic device, such as an iPhone or other mobile device. GPS systems add additional mobility to this information, permitting an ongoing feed of information to a mobile device that recalculates the journey when spontaneous changes in travel directions (e.g., detours) occur.

A geographical resource may also provide information related to a variety of specialized areas of information, including the study of environmental issues, regional planning, and historical and political events. For example, the *Atlas of World Political Flashpoints* provides geographic information about locations of conflict in the world as well as information about those conflicts. The *Atlas of Human Anatomy* provides location information in terms of the human body. In addition, there are a number of different travel guides, such as the *Lonely Planet* or *Eyewitness Travel Guide* series, that offer tourist information about hotels, restaurants, cultural sites, and contact information. Tourist guides may be published for a particular city, country, or geographic region and are indispensable in planning a vacation.

Second Life offers yet another form of geographical resource, enabling individuals to assume alternate identities as avatars and to participate in virtual communities. Concepts of latitude and longitude apply in this virtual world as coordinates for community destinations. Libraries, art exhibitions, college campuses, clubhouses, and similar locales are all created by the members of Second Life. Take a class, read a book, sail a ship, attend a meeting or seminar, meet new friends—anything is possible in the world you create or simply join.

Quick Tips: Adopting and Living a Second Life

How to sign up for a Second Life account:

1. Go to www.secondlife.com.
2. Select the *Join Now* button.
3. You may be prompted to join a community. Select the *Skip This Step* button for now.
4. Follow the on-screen instructions to create your avatar and obtain free Second Life software for your PC.
5. Launch the Second Life software on your PC.
6. Start living your Second Life.

Joining a Group: Many groups have free and open enrollment, such as the Science Center group. To join:

1. Select *Search* near the bottom of your Second Life window.
2. Select the *Groups* tab.
3. In the text-entry area, type *Science Center*
4. Select *Search*.
5. Select the *Science Center group* from the list of results.
6. Select the *Join* button.

YEARBOOKS

A yearbook provides facts and statistics for a single year. In addition, a yearbook may include a chronology for the year, biographies of newsmakers, obituaries, sports news, and so forth. A yearbook may function as a supplement to another type of information tool, for example, an encyclopedia. However, a yearbook may also stand alone as a publication. *Canada Yearbook* and the *Europa World Book* are examples of yearbooks, each of which is associated with particular information. For example, *Canada Yearbook*, now available on the Internet as *Canada e-Book*, http://142.206.72.67/ r000_e.htm, covers major events taking place in a particular year, as well as information about Canada's government structure, economy, culture, and history.

It is important to remember that the information contained in a given yearbook is generally a collection of facts and events related to the year preceding the date of publication. As a result, you must take this into account in your search strategy. Although more and more publications are widely available through the Internet, and electronic publications are theoretically more easily updated to provide the most current information available, you may still find that publications found in print and in electronic formats have similar levels of currency of information. As a result, do not assume that an electronic yearbook will provide the most current information available.

Tips on Incorporating Fact-Finding Tools Effectively into a Search

The number of tools we can use to locate factual information is endless. Understanding basic categories of these resources, keeping in mind the purpose and typical information content of a given resource type, and having firsthand experience with some of these resources are essential to developing a plan for locating factual information. However, it is equally important to remember that the process of locating this form of information is enabled by the structure of these sources. Combining a few specialized tips with a well-considered search plan will help you to navigate resources and locate factual information with greater ease.

First, given the factual information you wish to find, evaluate your starting point. What do you know already about this information that might help you? Consider the type of information you are hoping to find—for example, numerical information. In addition, have you had previous successful searches for this type of information? Our attempts to find information reinforce our patterns of information seeking. Remember the usual structure of the particular information you need and allow this to inform your choice of sources of information.

Suppose you have no idea where you might look for a given piece of information. Remember that handbooks, such as *Walford's*, are invaluable for outlining the types of resources, along with examples of publications, that cover particular forms of information. Keep in mind a hierarchy of resources. Recall that many resources of a similar type may be collected together. For instance, you may refer to a "dictionary of dictionaries" to identify individual dictionaries that are suitable to your search need. Start your search here to gather more information for your perfect search plan.

Consider efficiency, as well as effectiveness, in your search. Identify the category of tool that will most efficiently guide you to the information you need. Remember that two resources may provide similar information in content but perhaps by different routes. For example, suppose you need to know who Job was. We can identify the object of our information search as Job, and we may know that he is a biblical character. You might, therefore, assume that a Bible is the logical source to consult. However, will this strategy prove to be the most efficient route to the information you need? Biblical information is gathered in a variety of tools geared toward providing small bits of information; for example, a Bible dictionary will provide this sort of pointed information arranged alphabetically by topic or name. We need only look under J for Job in a resource, such as the *Anchor Bible Dictionary*, and we are likely to find a brief summary that details who Job was and why he is remembered. This is a more efficient approach than scanning line-by-line text in a large source like a Bible for a small bit of information. Once we have located our information about Job, we might then refer to the relevant section of a Bible for additional information related to this person or this period of time.

As you select different fact-finding resources, be sure to think about how each resource is organized. We know already that certain resources are arranged in particular ways. For example, encyclopedias list short articles in alphabetical order by topic. We might expect to find an index of alphabetically arranged place names along with degrees of longitude and latitude in an atlas. Individual entries in directories may list similar bits of information in a particular order, such as name, affiliation, street address, telephone number, e-mail address, website URL. Electronic versions of the same tools in print form may offer additional options, such as multimedia and electronic search functions. Although automated search functions may suggest that a tool is different, keep in mind that the structure of information within a tool often remains the same as in its print version. Many items are simply uploaded to the Internet. It remains important to consider the resource and its purpose, rather than format alone.

You should not assume that you know precisely how a given resource has been organized. Remember that, although types of fact-finding tools bear similarities that allow us to categorize them as handbooks, almanacs, and so on, individual publications may also differ in organization. For this reason, it is essential to read and refer to the front matter of a resource whenever you come across unfamiliar information within a tool. The initial pages in any of these publications function as a decoder ring for the publication, providing critical information, such as the meanings of abbreviations used within entries in the resource (for example, journal titles), an itemization of the contents of any given entry, and guidelines for using the resource. Without this information, you might not use the resource as effectively or efficiently as you might otherwise if you kept this information in mind.

Although a publication may fall into a particular category of factual information tool, remember that it is also a unique resource in terms of content. Publishers differ in policies for collecting types of information. For this reason, resources may cover different parts of a subject area and differ in amounts of detail or comprehensiveness. Differences in resources may mean that you need to consult more than one resource of a given type. In other words, if you are unable to locate a particular piece of information in one resource, try another one and you may succeed.

Evaluate the resources you consult. Would you opt to use this resource again? Why or why not? Our successes and failures in search outcomes with a particular resource may affect our willingness to return to a resource. However, the way in which the information has been arranged within the resource may also influence you to make a mental note to return to this resource to answer future information queries. Ease of use often contributes to an information-seeking pattern of taking the path of least effort. Remem-

Quick Tips for Finding Factual Information

- Identify the type of information you wish to find.
- Consider the ranges and types of potential sources of factual information for this type of information.
- Explore how these resources structure information or provide pathways to information.
- Use handbooks to build a strategy for finding the factual information needed.
- Remember helpful resources and build a collection of efficient and effective resources for future searching.

ber that fact-finding tools attempt to collect and systematize information in ways that facilitate this type of information-seeking behavior.

Exercise 1

1. What does SARS stand for? Think of another acronym and find it. Hint: What sort of electronic reference tool might help you search for acronyms? How can Internet homepages also be useful here?
2. Locate one of the reference tools noted in this chapter. Examine the front matter in this item in print or the About page online and describe how information is organized in this resource. Identify the individual steps you must follow to locate information in this tool.
3. Look for the subject of your choice in a general encyclopedia such as Britannica and then in Wikipedia, www.wikipedia.com. Compare and contrast the information you find in each resource and how this information has been compiled. Evaluate the benefits and drawbacks of using a traditionally published encyclopedia versus an encyclopedia like Wikipedia that has been compiled by volunteers.
4. What classes are taking place in Second Life now? When you start Second Life software, select the link for classes and make

a list of free classes scheduled for today. What other types of events are available? Use the calendar function to build a schedule of events for you to attend online.

Information Hunt

What reference tool would you use to answer the following questions? Be sure to start by identifying the factual information required to solve each information problem.

1. What is a hurricane?
2. Where is Newgrange located?
3. What events took place on the day you were born?
4. How old is author Stephen King?
5. What is the population of Australia?
6. Where would you find an obituary for Princess Grace of Monaco?
7. Where would you find a short summary of the life of Chu Yüan-chang?
8. What should you wear to a formal evening wedding?
9. What countries are crossed by the equator?
10. Who won the local ice skating championship last year?

Find the following in Second Life:

1. Is Mohawk College located on an island?
2. Join the Science Fiction group. Is there a charge to join this group?

Exercise 2: Building a Personal Resource Library

Using the following table as a starting point, begin a personal collection of your favorite online or printed tools for locating factual information. You may want to input your information into a file-saving and/or sharing platform such as Delicious, http://delicious.com, Endnote, or RefWorks to keep track of sources you might use again and again. You might even simply bookmark online sources using your Internet browser.

Your Resource Library

Type of Source	Definition	Organization	Example
Almanac	Provides factual info about a given year (e.g., calendar, astronomical info, political, historical, current events)		
Biographical Source	Provides information about people		
Dictionary	Provides definitions, pronunciation, etc. May have subject focus		
Encyclopedia	Provides summaries of factual information		
Directory	Provides a list of people and/or organizations		
Geographic Source (e.g., atlases, maps, GPS, travel guides)	Provides location information		
Handbook	Provides guidance on a particular topic		
Yearbook	Provides facts and statistics for a single year (e.g., chronology, biographies for newsmakers, obituaries, sports news)		

CHAPTER 4

Selecting and Navigating Electronic Information Systems

There are numerous electronic information resources we can explore in our quest for information. In fact, there are so many electronic resources of information available, both freely and with payment for use, that even identifying a tool can be a daunting task. It is essential to be able to select the appropriate electronic tool to accomplish the task at hand and, further, to mine that tool to maximize information retrieval, evaluate your overall search outcome, and be able to say with confidence that you have found what you need. In addition, you want to search efficiently, by developing such strategies as searching multiple databases simultaneously and scanning for new information on an ongoing basis.

A number of issues affect our success in navigating resources to find information. For example, a cost associated with using an electronic database may deter us from using this resource. Usability and friendliness of the system's interface, the functionality of the search engine, and ongoing changes to configurations of these parts of the system can all affect our confidence in our ability to use an electronic resource and to obtain the information we need or want to find. Even our own evaluation of our search results can affect our search success. We need to understand the mechanics of an electronic search, as well as the evaluation of our search outcome, including the authenticity and reliability of a resource or piece of information found.

This chapter helps you accomplish all of these goals by encouraging you to develop and practice your electronic search skills.

What You Will Learn in This Chapter

In this chapter, we focus on the world of electronic information, through which you will learn to do the following:

- Plan an effective electronic information search
- Identify electronic information resources
- Evaluate electronic information and electronic resources of information
- Compose a Boolean search string
- Become a super searcher by taking advantage of advanced search functions
- Evaluate search outcomes

Selecting an Electronic Resource for Your Query

Choosing the appropriate electronic resource can be a challenge. Although it has become fashionable to turn to search engines, such as Google, for answers to any and all questions in the online environment, there are actually numerous electronic resources that may be used to answer an information query, alone and in combination.

Identifying appropriate electronic resources to search involves careful matching of your information need or want to a resource that can effectively and efficiently provide the answer to your query. Be sure to consider each of the following selection criteria before you choose an electronic resource.

AVAILABLE RESOURCES TO HELP YOU SIFT THROUGH ELECTRONIC TOOLS

Different tools exist to help guide you through the process of selecting an electronic tool. Although individual database vendors provide lists of their products, it is useful to consult tools that outline resources compiled by a variety of producers. A commonly used resource is the *Gale Directory of Databases,* which itemizes electronic databases available worldwide in various electronic formats. Information provided about individual databases includes the name and contact details of the database producer, description of database content, access costs, and so on. This information can help you select databases to include in your searching. The Gale Directory of Databases is only one of the directories in the Gale Directory Library. Check your library's catalogue for a print copy or request a product trial at Gale's Directory Library website, www.gale.cengage.com/DirectoryLibrary. Other subject-specific tools may reveal a range of electronic resources for your search. For example, a gateway of vetted tools may also help you locate relevant information. The OMNI (Organising Medical Networked Information) gateway, http://omni.ac.uk, based at the University of Nottingham, provides access to Internet resources focused on the subject of health and medicine.

> The computer is only a fast idiot, it has no imagination; it cannot originate action. It is, and will remain, only a tool to man.
>
> —On Univac computer exhibited at the 1964 New York World's Fair, American Library Association

You may have a favorite database or search engine that you automatically choose for your searches. It is only natural for us to turn to those resources we have found helpful in the past. However, this is your opportunity to expand your array of electronic resources. Try something new!

COVERAGE

Investigate the coverage of an electronic resource before you search it. Your information query will help you identify whether or not a resource has suitable coverage. Areas such as subject, journal, geographic coverage, and time period must all be considered carefully so that you do not inadvertently omit searching relevant information. Remember to read the information provided about an electronic resource before you begin searching. This preliminary step will help you identify whether you should consult another resource instead or possibly multiple resources to make your search more comprehensive.

CURRENT AND UPDATED INFORMATION

Always establish the currency of the information you are about to use. Electronic resources usually provide, at minimum, the date on which the resource was created. The resource should also specify the creation date of the information contained in the product—for example, a range of publication dates of articles.

Be sure to identify the last time the product was updated and the frequency of updating. Take care with misleading information about updates as well; for instance, a date stamp on a web page may mean many things, including the current date on which you are visiting the site or the last time the overall site was checked. It is very possible that particular information on the site has not been updated, even though another aspect of the site has been modified and, therefore, the site appears to have been updated.

SEARCH OPTIONS

What search options are available to you in the particular resource you have chosen? Although you may be well versed with keyword searching, a more advanced search option is likely to provide you with greater control over your search outcome. Explore the search options available to you, and identify the basics as well as the advanced search options you might use.

Be aware of the subtle nuances of a search mechanism, which might not seem apparent at first glance. For example, are Boolean operators assumed in a search? That is, does the system add an operator whether or not you enter it into the search box? (Boolean operators are explained in greater detail in this chapter under the heading Boolean Basics.)

Are you also aware of the advanced system features that may facilitate your search for information? For example, depending on the product, you may have the option to save your searches through an alert option. In this case, the system will run your search periodically and advise you of any new information that has been added to the database. This function is very helpful, if you need to follow new developments in a subject area.

ORGANIZATION OF INFORMATION

The organization of information in the electronic resource you choose can facilitate or impede your search. Ask yourself the same questions you would of a printed resource: How has the information been presented? What sort of logical structure has been imposed on information in the resource?

Remember that every product is organized differently. The electronic resource may offer categorized information, filtered hierarchically into sections or folders by subject. Advanced searchers may expect to find information in the resource indexed so that a search for an indexing term will locate specific items on a given topic. (Indexing is discussed in greater detail in this chapter under the heading Controlled Vocabulary.) The resource may also simply provide hyperlinks to connect one topic logically to another related topic.

USER-FRIENDLINESS

System interface can make or break your search experience. We expect the system to be user-friendly, that is, relatively easy to use whether we have used the interface before or not. When you approach a system interface, explore the system thoroughly and identify any areas that might be more challenging to use effectively. Is there a Help option to help you navigate this product more effectively and efficiently? Preparation is key to your successful interaction with the system interface. Make sure you are aware of what the system can do for you and then maximize this potential!

RELIABILITY

Remember to consider the content of the electronic resource you plan to use. Always assess the accuracy of information contained in a resource, and verify information you find with that found in another resource. It is essential that you are able to trust the content of the electronic resource you select. For example, it is possible to locate the periodic table on the Internet at different websites, but be careful! Depending on the site you choose, you may find a periodic table that is missing elements.

AUTHORITY

Always ensure that the electronic resource you select has been produced by an authoritative source. Evaluate the resource, using the same high standards you use when considering other forms of information. Do not be fooled into believing that information is automatically credible just because it has been supplied in electronic format. Remember that "Bob's Homepage" might look appealing and may seem to provide lots of information, but this source of information may not provide reliable content and may lack the necessary authority to give that information credibility. Even a resource we might feel inclined to trust may present biased information. For example, a business website is much more likely to encourage you to purchase its products rather than suggest reasons why you should not purchase from that business.

Some simple guidelines can help you determine the authoritativeness of an electronic resource. Start by examining the resource for the name of an author or producer. Then investigate this person's or entity's credentials. For Internet resources, the URL can help indicate the authority of the resource. URLs with extensions of .edu or .gov are generally considered to have greater authority because the pages are hosted by educational institutions (.edu) or government bodies (.gov). Smith (2005) suggests checking the ownership of a domain name through a WHOIS service (e.g., www .internic.net/whois.html), which allows you to identify URL extensions by country and search for domain names.

WEIGHING THE PROS AND CONS OF ONE RESOURCE OVER ANOTHER

Finally, as you explore the many electronic resources available to you, keep in mind your reasons for choosing a resource. Can you identify particular advantages this product has over other electronic resources? What advantages does one electronic resource have over the equivalent resource in another format?

Creating a Search Query: Getting Our Message to the System

How can two people pursuing the same information in the same database achieve different results? Differing results can arise for a number of reasons.

Remember, we need to be prepared for our search. Our information status as we embark on a search, including our understanding of our search problem as well as our ability to manipulate an information system, will play a critical role in our progress with our interaction with an electronic resource. Preparing to meet both challenges will help us reduce possible uncertainty or anxiety about the search.

It is important that we think about our approach to an electronic information system. Although many electronic information systems have increased user-friendliness over the past several years, using an electronic resource for the first time can still feel intimidating. However, the pressures of time may make you feel that you must forge ahead. Familiarity with other electronic resources and the identification of similarities between resources, even at a superficial level, may also make resources appear the same in function, although the behind-the-scenes workings of the resource may be quite different.

There is a young and impressionable mind out there that is hungry for information. It has latched onto an electronic tube as its main source of nourishment.

—Joan Ganz Cooney (1929–)

Quick Tips Summary: How to Choose Electronic Resources

Be sure to answer the following questions when you select an electronic tool:

- Have you chosen the most efficient route to the information you need? For example, is the same source available in another format that can be more easily or quickly accessed?
- Is there a list of databases that can help you locate appropriate tools for your search?
- What is the coverage of this electronic resource?
- Is this electronic resource current? How frequently is it updated?
- How has this electronic resource been organized?
- How easy is the electronic resource to use? Do you need specialized systems knowledge to use this resource effectively?
- How is this electronic tool searched?
- How reliable is this electronic resource?
- What is the authenticity of this electronic resource?
- Why have you chosen this particular electronic resource?

A common approach among less-experienced searchers is to locate the search box for the resource and enter a question in its entirety, such as *Why is the sky blue?* This approach was extremely popular with Ask Jeeves, now Ask.com since the butler, Jeeves, retired. The basics of searching, including the use of logical search operators, however, did not really disappear. Search mechanisms select words from the text entered, even long sentences and phrases, and include these in a search string to mine the resource's store of information automatically.

Since logical operators are still very much part of searching an electronic resource, it is worthwhile reviewing their function and use here.

BOOLEAN BASICS

Boolean operators, created by mathematician George Boole (1815–1864), enable us to communicate our search queries to a system. The search operators NOT, AND, and OR provide the basics of search logic for our queries.

OR

Use the OR operator to widen your search. Try to begin your construction of a Boolean search query by considering the terms you might "OR" together. In this way, you can cast your information net widely, envisioning the potential range of information that might be found in a search. Then you can manipulate your search outcome by using AND and NOT to narrow your search.

For example, if you wanted to find information about young people, you might use *youth* as a search term. However, to increase your chances of locating items relevant to your search query, you should also consider alternative ways of expressing this concept in your search. For example, you are likely to find more items by altering your search string to reflect the different ways in which authors might refer to this age group in their work. Make a list of all the synonyms for young people: for example, adolescent, teenager, juvenile. Then create a search string incorporating these terms, as follows:

youth or adolescent or teenager or juvenile

Your search outcome will contain works with any, some, or all of these terms in the fields of the records searched.

AND

The AND operator is used to narrow a search, that is, to focus your search outcome on the criteria you specify. A search for

crime and cities

will produce a search outcome, in which items found contain both search terms.

Once you have expressed concepts in groups of terms connected by the OR operator, you can look for the items that overlap among these groups. For example, you might search for youth and crime in cities as follows:

(youth or adolescent or teenager or juvenile) and crime and cities

In this case, our search for terms about youth is executed first, because of the parentheses around this part of the search. The result of this part of the search is then combined with the remaining search terms and the intersection of these three subsets of records becomes your final search outcome.

NOT

The NOT operator, when it is available, is used to exclude items containing particular search terms from your search results. For example, if you wished to search a database for items mentioning citrus fruits, including oranges and lemons but not grapefruits, you might try the following Boolean search string:

"citrus fruits" not grapefruits

Note that the quotation marks denote *citrus fruits* as a phrase. In this case, a search engine will search for the words *citrus* and *fruits* together as one entity. Alternatively, you might name the fruits you wished to find:

(oranges or lemons) not grapefruits

In either case, the NOT operator excludes items mentioning grapefruits from your search results. For example, the second search string would locate items mentioning either oranges or lemons, but not grapefruits.

It is important to note here that items mentioning oranges or lemons as well as grapefruits will be excluded from your search results. If your goal is actually to gather information about citrus fruits, such as oranges and lemons, comprehensively, it may prove counterproductive to exclude one type of fruit from your search. With the NOT operator, there is a real danger of excluding relevant and even important information from your search results; therefore, it is wise to use the NOT operator sparingly. Like salt and pepper added to a fine meal, a little goes a long way to enhance the flavor of the food.

Order of Operations

Always remember that the accepted order of performing these operations is NOT, AND, and then OR. Note, for example, the difference between the following two search strings:

lavender or rosemary and tonic

versus

(lavender or rosemary) and tonic

In the first search string, the term *tonic* will be combined only with the term *rosemary* in our search. To search for works that contain tonic and either lavender or rosemary, then we must tell the system to search for the terms *lavender* and *rosemary* first and then combine this result with the term *tonic*, as we have done in the second search string above. When in doubt about the order of a set of operations, use parentheses to dictate the order to the system.

Always remember that the search function in a given electronic resource will make use of Boolean operators in retrieving material for you, possibly employing certain automatic Boolean functions, although the terminology used to express particular search operations may differ from resource to resource. For example, under advanced search options, you are unlikely to need to enter a search string in its entirety; instead, you will often see a series of search options that represent the Boolean logic operators, but presented as explanatory phrases. For instance, the AND search operation may be represented by the phrase *must have* or *contains*

Blogspot: Google's Advanced Search

While Google offers a simple search on its opening page, it also offers an advanced search option. Advanced search features translate to the Boolean operators and search devices we have reviewed.

Find pages that have
   All these words . . .   translates to the AND search operator
   This exact wording or phrase . . .   translates to a phrase search noted by
                                      quotation marks, e.g., "cotton wool"
   One or more of these words . . .   translates to the OR search operator

But don't show pages that have
   Any of these unwanted words . . .   translates to the NOT search operator

Search for a topic of your own using both Google's simple search and advanced search options. Write about each search experience in your blog, noting the advantages of each search option.

all of these words, while the NOT operation may be expressed as *must not have* or *contains none of these words.* The OR operation may be expressed as *contains some of these words* or *contains any of these words.*

EXPLOITING SEARCH FACILITIES

Although we may be anxious to get on with the search and therefore be tempted just to type search terms into search boxes, remember that you can improve your search with some simple additional search specifications. Be sure to remember that Internet search engines as well as databases apply these techniques.

The search options noted below represent only a few of the techniques that may be available for your use. There are many search features to explore, including searching by domain name or URL, searching by type of media (e.g., mp3, images, video), searching by file format, and limiting your search by time period, language, or number range. Always explore the Search Help facility for any search function to ensure you are fully aware of the search possibilities and the means of representing each option that may be particular to a given electronic resource.

Truncation

Truncation enables you to search for a word in more than one form. For example, a search for *rational** can locate *rational, rationale,* and *rationalization*. You can also use truncation to capture pluralization in the middle of words, such as wom*n. You may be able to set the number of letters to be allowed in the truncated part of a word, for example, encyclop2*dia. The actual truncation symbol may vary from resource to resource—for example, * or ?—so be sure to consult the Help facility for a given resource before you truncate search terms.

However, take care with how you truncate a word. A search for *cat** can locate *cat, cats, catastrophe, catalogue, catalyst,* and many more. If you are really looking for the furry feline, then you should revise your search. Some search facilities will allow you to search for plurals only, using a specialized truncation symbol, which would better suit your search in this case.

Proximity Searching

In addition to phrase searching, in which you search for a group of words enclosed in quotation marks, you may be able to search for words adjacent to one another. For example, a search for *apple with pie* or *apple (w) pie* will locate the two words next to each other and in the word order apple and then pie. Similarly, *apple (n) pie* will find the two words together but in any order. *Apple (4n) pie* will locate the two words within four words of each other and in any order. Again, the symbols to use when searching for words beside or near each other may vary from resource to resource.

Search Alerts and Current Awareness Services

A search alert facility offers you ongoing benefits from the search you have created by enabling you to save your search string to use again in future. The alert service can be set to run your search periodically and report results back to you via e-mail. Make sure you check to see whether a given electronic resource, especially databases and journal services, offers a search alert function.

In addition, you may wish to consult a current awareness service. This type of service provides continuous information about recent developments in an area of interest to you. Once you have signed up for a current awareness service and have selected the publications you wish to monitor, you will be contacted periodically with tables of contents for newly issued items, such as journals and patents. Many services also offer document delivery, so that you may request items you wish to read from your alert or current awareness list and have these delivered in your chosen format.

Controlled Vocabulary

Some databases have used indexers to assign controlled vocabulary terms to represent topics found in the items contained in a database. The assigned terms taken together are referred to as a controlled vocabulary and constitute an artificial language, one that we would not speak but would use to communicate our search requirements to a search engine. Examples of controlled vocabulary include subject heading lists, thesauri, and hierarchical classification schemes.

The assigned controlled vocabulary or indexing terms may be searched to retrieve items from a database about a particular topic. In addition to the search terms you think of on your own, also often referred to as natural language, a controlled vocabulary search, when available, can add great power to your searching because the terms have been attached to items by information professionals. The U.S. National Library of Medicine, for example, has developed a very large database of indexed articles using its own controlled vocabulary.

Knowing when to opt for controlled vocabulary, natural language, or a combination of the two is important to retrieving the desired results from a resource. For instance, controlled vocabulary searching can help you pinpoint the items in a database that largely focus on your topic. To increase your number of search hits, gathering even marginally relevant items, you should add natural language to create a more comprehensive search. Remember that natural language will also help you capture nuances in meaning and new terms that do not yet exist in the controlled vocabulary, such as new medical terms for conditions.

Combing the Internet for Information

Many databases and electronic services are now easily accessed for free or a fee through the web. Using a search engine, you should, in theory, be able to access an infinite amount of information. In the previous section, we reviewed some of the search features available in electronic resources generally, including Internet search engines. Here are a few tips to keep in mind for your next web search.

REV UP YOUR SEARCH ENGINE

Remember, when searching the web, that search engines may differ in terminology used and in search algorithms applied to your search queries. Although Google, Yahoo!, and MSN are known ubiquitously, veteran searchers will also recall and use Ask, AlltheWeb, AltaVista, and others. Be sure to explore the background for the service you choose; for example, you might be surprised to learn that AltaVista uses Yahoo!'s search database. Monitor *Search Engine Watch*, http://searchenginewatch.com, for up-to-date information on your favorite search engine. And remember to venture beyond your usual search engine choice on the web and note the differences in your search results.

> *I'm a doctor, not a database.*
>
> —The Doctor, *Star Trek: Voyager,* "Future's End: Part 2" (Season 3, Episode 9, 1995)

Blogspot: Practicing Our Search Skills

For each of the search problems listed below, conduct an advanced Google search for information. Now try the same searches using the advanced search features of at least two other search engines:

1. Affordable traveling board games for young people
2. Spam blockers that really work
3. Careers in bodybuilding among women
4. Risk factors associated with high-level dosages of Vitamin E
5. Success rates in optical laser surgery

Write about your search experience in your blog. How do your search results vary from one search engine to another? Which search engine would you use again? Why?

One means of overcoming the difficulty of choosing a single search engine to use, especially when we know that different search engines produce differing results, is to try our search in a parallel or meta search engine. Dogpile, www.dogpile.com, Vivisimo, http://vivisimo.com, and Mamma, aka the Mother of All Search Engines, www.mamma.com, represent only a few of the meta search engines available to you. These meta search engines will run your search in multiple search engines at once, using the data compiled by other search engines to locate an answer for your query.

ANALYZING SEARCH RESULTS FROM AN ELECTRONIC RESOURCE

Now that you have completed your search, let's review your search results. A close inspection of your search results will enable you to decide whether you should revise your current search approach, devise a new search, or end your search at this time. Take some time now and examine your search results carefully.

Several factors determine our satisfaction with a search. Depending on your original reason for consulting an electronic resource, you may value certain aspects of your search more than others. For example, if your original intention was to produce a comprehensive search on a topic, you will expect your search to produce as many hits as possible about your topic. For any search outcome, however, consider the number of items you have located. Regardless of the motivation for the search, the number of search hits should be manageable. If your search has produced more items than you can reasonably review, then you should consider a revised or different search. The problem of overwhelming numbers of results is particularly difficult to control when searching the web. In this circumstance, searchers generally accept that even the most carefully composed search is likely to produce thousands and even millions of search hits. To avoid feelings of information overload, searchers often then limit their review of search hits to the first few pages of search results.

> To win by strategy is no less the role of a general than to win by arms.
>
> —Julius Caesar, 100–44 BCE

Particularly with information located through the web, evaluate the reliability of the information you have found, as well as the authority of

Quick Tips Summary: Evaluating Your Search Results from an Electronic Resource

How would you rate your search results? Consider the following points as you analyze your search results.

- How many items has your search uncovered? Is this number manageable or overwhelming?
- How reliable is the information you have located?
- What is the authority for the information you have located?
- Is this information current? If you wanted retrospective information, have you found this information as well as recently published information?
- What sort of information have you found?
- Does this information satisfy your information query?

this information. Remember that currency is important; always look for dates of publication or updates. Older information may also be relevant, if your search motivation was a retrospective search for information on a given topic. In any case, determine the nature of the information you find and evaluate whether the information satisfies your original information query.

—⁂—

Exercise

1. Using the Internet, locate NordGuide, a directory of databases in the Nordic countries. What are the criteria for inclusion of a database in this directory? Given the date of the last revision of this directory, what would you do to supplement the information you have found here?
2. Check your local public library or your university library for lists of electronic resources provided to users. Hint: This information may be found through the library's portal to information on the Internet.

3. What is a *Google Whack*? Search for this concept on the Internet. Then see if you can develop a Google Whack of your own. Why is the result of a Google Whack significant?

Electronic Information Hunt

For each of the following search problems, remember to build a search strategy by identifying concepts, search terms, appropriate databases, and search strings. Then try your search using different electronic resources and compare your results from each resource.

1. Where can you locate dessert recipes that list garlic as a key ingredient?
2. Where can you find information about speech-recognition software?
3. What items can you find about the use of shark cartilage to fight cancer?
4. Where might you locate items about the strength of copper cookware? How many items can you find?
5. What information can you find about white wines produced in South American countries?
6. How has soil erosion affected the coastline in the United Kingdom?
7. What items can you find about the effects of Vitamins A or B on immune systems?
8. How would you go about booking a holiday online, including travel, lodgings, and entertainment?
9. Where can you find reliable information about coffee production in the world?
10. What are the game rules for cricket?

CHAPTER 5

Practices of Information Organization and Access

We have a habit of organizing information to different degrees and following different approaches. How is information best organized to facilitate our finding it? We might reason that a quick Internet search provides an overwhelming list of results, opening a world of information to the searcher, so what advantages are there to organizing information? This chapter considers means of information organization and nonorganization and the usefulness and appropriateness of each approach in our lives. In particular, we examine these issues through two commonly used web-based approaches to organizing information to facilitate easy access: WorldCat and Google Books.

What You Will Learn in This Chapter

In this chapter, we focus on how we organize and do not organize information. By considering options for organizing information, you will learn to do the following:

- Consider the role of organization of information in our lives
- Compare traditional and new forms of managing information
- Apply systems or methods of organizing information to solve everyday information problems effectively

Traditional Forms of Organization of Information

BIBLIOGRAPHIC CONTROL

Bibliographic control has long governed how we manage information in our everyday lives. The word *bibliographic* comes from *biblios*, which is Greek for books. Bibliographic control involves the gathering and organizing of information in a systematic fashion to facilitate its location at another time. Bibliographic control is established and maintained through essential tools, including bibliographies, catalogues, and indexes. Each of these tools generally provides indirect access to materials by giving us a description or bibliographic reference to a full item. This reference may contain only the basics, such as author, title, and source, or, with ongoing enhancement of digital systems, might also offer an abstract,

> *Stardate 9521.6. Captain's Log, USS Excelsior. Hikaru Sulu commanding. After three years, I have concluded my first assignment as master of this vessel, cataloguing gaseous planetary anomalies in Beta Quadrant. We're heading home under full impulse power.*
>
> —Captain Hikaru Sulu, *Star Trek VI, The Undiscovered Country*, 1991

subject or descriptor terms, table of contents, and more, depending on the type of resource. These references are collected together to enable us to determine whether or not a needed resource exists in that collection or in a publication pertaining to a given subject area.

In addition to the concept of bibliographic control, there is also universal bibliographic control. When writer Douglas Adams coined the phrase, "life, the universe, and everything" in The Hitchhiker's Guide to the Galaxy series, he summed up the aim of universal bibliographic control. This is bibliographic control that extends beyond your library to the world of information. Universal bibliographic control attempts to provide access to information at an international level, using internationally recognized bibliographic standards. In both cases, the nature of bibliographic control remains to establish and maintain standards of describing and organizing information. The International Federation of Library Associations and Institutions (IFLA) and the Conference of Directors of National Libraries

(CDNL) work together to develop bibliographic standards through the IFLA-CDNL Alliance for Digital Strategies (ICADS), www.ifla.org/en/icads. In response to the increasing prevalence of digital resources, this group now focuses its efforts on digital libraries.

THREE TRADITIONAL FORMS OF BIBLIOGRAPHIC CONTROL

You may wonder how you would spot evidence of bibliographic control in your daily interactions with information. Bibliographies, catalogues, and indexes (or indices) offer three common forms of bibliographic control that you may have seen.

Bibliography and Documenting Published Literatures

A bibliography is an alphabetical list of items pertaining to a given subject area or type of material. Each item contains a reference or pointer to the full book, article, or other material related to the subject covered. As well as appearing at the end of a book or article, bibliographies are published on their own.

Bibliographies can take different forms. For instance, a subject bibliography, such as the *Bibliography of African Literatures*, provides a guide to a specific subject area. Trade bibliographies list books that are available from publishers, including such details for items as complete title, full author information, and price, but not including evaluation of the items. For example, *British Books in Print*, produced by J. Whitaker & Sons, lists books and audio materials published in the United Kingdom or published elsewhere in English and made available for purchase in the United Kingdom through a particular agent. Finally, national bibliographies cover items about a country or geographic region, such as *Canadiana: The National Bibliography of Canada*, www.collectionscanada.ca/canadiana/index-e.html.

Finding a bibliography is often considered a daunting task. However, the steps in finding a bibliography are often actually straightforward. Specific tools exist to assist you in your search for a bibliography. For example, bibliographies may be found through a *bibliography of bibliographies*. This type of bibliography gathers together in a list the names and references for different bibliographies on a particular topic, for example, *Parapsychology Foundation Bibliography No. 2: Bibliography of Bibliographies*, www .parapsychology.org/dynamic/info/pfbib2.pdf. However, bear in mind that while a bibliography of bibliographies offers a useful starting point for exploration, it remains essential to look at multiple sources to be comprehensive in locating relevant items.

Catalogues and Collections of Materials

A catalogue lists the items that form a collection. A description, or surrogate, is created for each item; surrogate records can then be searched to identify a particular item and locate its physical location within the collection. We are all familiar with printed and electronic catalogues of commercial goods. For instance, the database of materials at Amazon .com is essentially a catalogue of items presented for sale. Similarly, information centers and libraries supply a catalogue to provide staff and library patrons with access to items within the collection of materials held there.

Information centers and libraries most often offer their catalogue in electronic format as an OPAC, or Online Public Access Catalogue, publically accessible by either a computer terminal within the institution or through their website. However, some libraries have retained card catalogues and book catalogues that are still in use, in the process of retrospective catalogue conversion to electronic format or preserved for historical importance. Catalogues may vary in options offered to the user, but basic search mechanisms, such as author, title, and subject, are invariably present. Some institutions also work cooperatively to provide access across their collections by linking or integrating their catalogues. For example, the British Library offers an Integrated Catalogue, http://catalogue.bl.uk/F/?func=file&file_name=login -bl-list, to provide access to all of its collections.

> We still need your help. I just downloaded this. That's a catalog of over ten million people's DNA. We're looking for someone specific, a man.
>
> —Irina Derevko, *Alias*, 2001

Remember, a library catalogue is specific to a particular collection. In other words, do not assume that you have done a thorough search for an item if you have only checked one catalogue. The item you wish to find may be located in another collection and, therefore, in another catalogue. Importantly, this means that an appropriate question to pose to the catalogue in a library is "Does the library have this item?" However, the question "Does this item exist?" is *not* appropriate, since a library's collection may not have the item requested.

Indexes and Periodical Literature

As well as books, periodical literature can provide an important addition to a piece of writing. Knowing how to navigate this area of publication effectively is essential for gathering materials efficiently. As the name implies, periodical literature includes publications that appear serially, such as journals and newspapers. These publications may appear routinely, including daily, weekly, monthly, and annually, or even irregularly. Remember, these publications will have an International Standard Serial Number (ISSN) that uniquely identifies the publication's title, as well as volume and issue numbers, to denote publications under that title.

Indexes or indices offer a means of organizing periodical literature. An index is a pointing device that lists key attributes about an item we can use to refer to the actual item.

We can use a particular resource to help us find different databases of indexed items, whether periodical literature or other works. A standard, international bibliographic tool dedicated to documenting periodical publications is *Ulrich's Periodicals Directory*, www.ulrichsweb.com, published since 1932. *Ulrich's* maintains a comprehensive resource in which publishers' participation is free and encouraged. Because the tool is consulted by information professionals around the globe, it is in a publisher's best interests to have serial titles listed here. *Ulrich's* is available through subscription from Cambridge Scientific Abstracts (CSA), although a listing of newly added serials titles, title cessations, title changes, and mergers is updated monthly and made freely available via *Ulrich's* homepage.

Why should you use a tool like *Ulrich's*? Whether you access *Ulrich's Periodicals Directory* online or in print as *Ulrich's International Periodicals Directory* in your library, this resource can help you resolve different sorts of information problems. For example, you might want to publish a piece yourself in a serial publication. You can establish a list of potential publication venues through *Ulrich's*. Here is a sample information problem:

Information Problem: I would like to find the latest news on chemical engineering. I've heard that there are newsletters on this subject.
Information to Locate: Newsletters about chemical engineering

   Step 1: Remember that any type of serially published item may be found in *Ulrich's*, including newsletters. With that information, we can look up our subject, chemical engineering, at www.ulrichsweb.com.
   Step 2: Using Ulrichsweb's quick search or advanced search options, enter the search terms *chemical engineering* as a subject search, combined with the title keyword, *newsletter*.
   Step 3: Scan the list of newsletters about chemical engineering. Select some titles to view.

Twists on Organizing Information

Although bibliographic standards remain central to discussion about how best to organize information, the digital world continues to change and shape how we manage information. The highly participatory Web 2.0 environment has enabled us all to engage directly with information in new ways. Information resources have adopted techniques and trends from both traditional practices and new means of organizing information. To illustrate, let's take a closer look at two major resources: WorldCat and Google Books.

WORLDCAT

WorldCat, www.worldcat.org, is an international network of libraries, enabling one-stop searching for materials held in collections physically located around the world. WorldCat offers an easy-to-use interface, with simple searching as well as advanced searching. For instance, a search for the title *Cesar's Way* returns a list of items, including books, audiobooks, and videos, accompanied by bibliographic details. If we select the hyperlinked title for *Cesar's Way: The Natural, Everyday Guide to Understanding and Correcting Common Dog Problems*, we find greater detail about this particular book, including author links to further information about Cesar Millan and Melissa Jo Peltier, subject headings assigned to the item, and a content summary.

Advanced search features allow searching by ISBN or ISSN, as well as by Online Computer Library Center (OCLC) database accession number. Searches can be limited, for example, by language, format of material, and publication year. WorldCat also supports cloud tags, and you can add terms to describe an item and facilitate our searching for the item.

Once you have identified a title, you can locate a physical copy of the item by entering your location (postal code, state/province, or country) into the search box labeled *Borrow or Obtain a Copy*. The system will return a list of locations nearest the one you have searched for. Choose the link for one and the details for libraries holding the item will appear. Follow the link for one library's name and go directly to their catalogue entry for this item. You will then be able to see whether the item is in or out on loan, call number, number of copies in this collection, and so on, as you would if you were searching that catalogue directly.

Increasing visibility of its collections via the Internet, WorldCat also supports searching for items through Google and Yahoo! search engines. By including either the phrase *"Find in a Library"* (including the quotation marks), or *site:worldcatlibraries.org* (without a space after the colon), you will limit your search to items held by libraries that belong to WorldCat. Using Google or Yahoo! can yield different results, because the search engines use varying sets of information from WorldCat.

GOOGLE BOOKS

Google Books proposes to fulfill a similar function, enabling Internet searchers to locate books and further to create their own libraries or subsets of the materials collected by Google Books.

Google collaborated with some libraries to digitize their collections for its Google Books Library Project; however, controversy arose over copyright issues connected with scanning and disseminating published works. Following a class action lawsuit by authors and publishers in the United States, the Google Book Search Copyright Class Action Settlement was reached. Google states its primary goal is to facilitate access to books. However, their

Blogspot: Google Books and WorldCat

Using Google Books, http://books.google.com, and then WorldCat, www
.worldcat.org, search for *Alice's Adventures in Wonderland*, published by
Scholastic in 2002.

What library near you holds this book? To what service does Google
Books direct you for this information?

Writing in your blog, reflect on your search, comparing and contrast-
ing the information available about the book in Google Books and World-
Cat. For example, where can you find the full text? A review of the book?

proposed plan of charging fees for viewing materials has met with criticism
for constraining access to works in the public domain. In addition, public
libraries have long provided free access to materials. The situation has high-
lighted the potential for problems in digitization projects.

On the other hand, Google Books also provides an exciting opportunity for searchers keen to explore texts beyond the boundaries of traditional
mechanisms for providing access to information, such as catalogues. At
present, Google Books, http://books.google.com, offers both keyword and
advanced searching for books, based on its Google web search algorithm.
In addition to searching, you can select from Google's book categories to
view books. Retrieved items are displayed as either book cover view or list
view, which offers both book cover and some brief descriptive information
about the book. Although advertised as a card catalogue, the details provided vary from usual bibliographic descriptions to include author(s), title,
year of publication, genre, and very short description of content. Selecting
a book takes you to a preview area, where you can access usual publication details about the book, including number of pages. You can search
within the book's text for particular passages, find the book in a library,
or purchase the book from an online bookstore. Utilizing other developed
standards of bibliographic control, such as an International Standard
Book Number (ISBN) or Library of Congress Control Number (LCCN),
Google Books provides searching by these numbers to locate specific edi-
tions of a book. The system has even incorporated OCLC record numbers
to facilitate edition searching.

Similar to WorldCat's lists, Google Books enables personalized book
list or library building, which you can create and share with others. You

can rank books, annotate items, and write your own reviews. In Google Books, all of these features are viewable by the public.

The Ongoing Development of Organization of Information

We might initially wonder whether such tools as bibliographies, catalogues, and indexes continue to hold relevance to our information worlds. With the development of tools that promote individualized searching of the information "heap," is it still necessary to organize information? What are the limits of organizing information? On the other hand, can we really depend upon search engines to tame disorder by pulling relevant information from the proverbial haystack?

It would seem that even new initiatives recognize traditional notions of organizing information. Remember, Google Books encourages us to think of content around books as card catalogue information to help us visualize the information provided in a context with which we are familiar. WorldCat, although actually a long-time international cataloguing effort, has evolved to adopt new participatory options, bringing the collections of libraries worldwide to a wider public through the Internet and Web 2.0 devices. The movement toward integrated, interwoven information options suggests we have an exciting, fast-changing digital future ahead.

> *If you don't find it in the index, look very carefully through the entire catalogue.*
>
> —Sears, Roebuck, and Co., *Consumer's Guide*, 1897

—〰—

Exercise: Information Hunt

Use WorldCat to locate the following information:

1. Locate the item entitled *Expectations of Modernity: Myths and Meanings of Urban Life on the Zambian Copperbelt*. Who

authored this book? What library holds this book in its collection? Now locate this item using the *Find in a Library* function in the Yahoo! Search engine.

2. Locate Jane Austen's *Northanger Abbey*. Do any libraries in the Netherlands hold this book in sound recording format? Now locate this item using the *Find in a Library* function in Google's search engine.

3. What album title do musicians Harry Connick and George Michael have in common? What type of music is featured on each album?

4. What subject headings have been assigned to *The Scarlet Pimpernel*? Select the hyperlink for one of these subject headings. What are some of the other titles linked to this same subject heading?

5. In which year was Danica McKellar's *Math Doesn't Suck: How to Survive Middle-School Math without Losing Your Mind or Breaking a Nail* published?

6. What book has Sanjeev Bhaskar authored that contains his name in the title?

7. Using WorldCat's advanced search, find the title of an album recorded by the Pigeon Detectives. Have any other musicians recorded albums with the same title?

8. Find an article about Facebook written by Michael J. Bugeja. Export the bibliographic citation for this article to an Endnote library file. Use WorldCat and then Endnote to view the bibliographic citation in MLA format for this article.

9. Locate a sample of the text of Stef Penney's novel *The Tenderness of Wolves*. Who provided this sample text for WorldCat?

10. Find the book *Michelle Obama: First Lady of Hope*. Now search Google Books for the same title. When was this book published?

CHAPTER 6

Channels of Communication

Information comes to us in many forms. In addition to the traditional publication of information in book form, information can appear in an array of electronic and printed formats and as different types of publications. It is important to distinguish among forms of publication to evaluate the authority and reliability of information we intend to use. To understand how to locate information published through formal and informal channels, we need to know how information is packaged and communicated to individuals and communities. In this chapter, we explore some formal and informal processes of publication and how these processes facilitate our access to information.

What You Will Learn in This Chapter

In this chapter, we focus on the means by which information is generated and placed in the public domain through formal and informal channels. By studying different publication processes, you will learn to do the following:

- Identify formal and informal sources and means of communication
- Trace the paths by which a literature is generated and managed through specific information processes and communities
- Evaluate information channels
- Adopt appropriate information channels to solve information problems

Mechanisms for Information Access and Exchange

Information may be passed through formal and informal channels. Formal channels usually involve recognized means of production of information. Informal sources of information are usually not standard forms of publishing information.

Formal sources are those information resources over which bibliographic control has been exercised. In other words, formal resources of information can be identified and located through recognized means of organizing information. Formal sources range from dictionaries and encyclopedias to research reports published in journal articles and books.

Informal sources of information are just the opposite; that is, they are not usually published through traditional publication channels or part of a system of information control. For example, our friends and relatives can function as informal sources of information, providing us with various bits of information from other sources and their own experience. Even with the best of intentions, informal sources of information may not always be comprehensive or accurate; as a result, you should take care with the use to which you put an informal source. For example, formal sources, such as refereed journal articles, are preferred for academic writing, whereas "Joe's homepage" is a source of opinion.

It is important to note that, while one or the other means of communication or type of information source may be appropriate in a particular information context, both formal and informal communication have roles to play in our information worlds.

The Traditional, Formal Publication Process

Information published through established, formal channels, such as an academic publishing house or the popular press, generally follows a set path from the inception of a project to its dissemination in a public forum (see figure 6.1).

We normally think of this cycle as beginning with one or more authors who take an idea and write about it. For example, a fiction author writes a

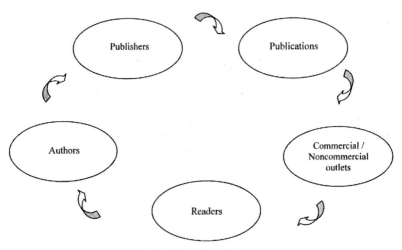

Figure 6.1.   The Formal Cycle of Publication

new best-seller or an article for a popular magazine. The author negotiates a contract with a publisher and the work is published. The author is the creative force behind the work. Publishers facilitate the production of the work as a book or other publication, including printing and distribution of the work. Publishing houses are usually linked to the nature of a work; for example, an academic publisher is likely to publish manuscripts relevant to a scholastic audience, ranging from schools to universities, while a popular press may publish novels and nonfiction works.

When a publishing house prepares a work for publication, it provides various functions that assist in future identification and location of the work. For example, publishers assign a unique number to each work they publish. In the case of books, this number is called an ISBN, or International Standard Book Number. The assignment of the ISBN—or ISSN (International Standard Serials Number) in the case of a magazine or other periodical literature—to a work provides a critical link in the formal chain of communication here, because this unique identifier enables us to distinguish a particular work from others that may appear to be similar.

Publishers also commonly liaise with national ventures to provide pre-publication cataloguing information in the front matter of manuscripts before they are published. Publishers in a given country work cooperatively with libraries to provide Cataloguing in Publication (CIP) information in books. Publishers notify customers and booksellers in advance of forth-coming publications, providing CIP data in publication lists, including publishers' catalogues of items available for purchase. As works are published or are about to be published, bibliographic information is also added to databases, such as *Books in Print*, in individual and collected reviews of works. It is worth noting here that individuals may elect to self-publish, including obtaining an ISBN and arranging inclusion in bibliographic databases, through an imprint service. By doing so, this type of self-publishing or vanity press venture maintains a connection with formal communication channels.

> *The moment a man sets his thoughts down on paper, however secretly, he is in a sense writing for publication.*
>
> —Raymond Chandler
> (1888–1959)

Once production of the work is complete, the item must be distributed to the public. This stage may involve commercial or noncommercial outlets. For instance, you might visit a local bookstore and select this work from the items on display for purchase. Perhaps you'll shop for the work online through an online bookstore, for example, the well-known Amazon.com. You might also obtain the work free of charge through a noncommercial outlet, for example, borrowed from a public library or received from a volunteer organization. In addition, distribution of works via the Internet has become increasingly popular, with publishing bodies making works available in abstract and full-text formats. In some cases, electronic distribution is provided at no expense to the consumer, although some types of literature, such as e-books, are available by subscription.

Although the publication cycle seems simple and straightforward, the process may be interrupted or delayed at any stage. In addition, feedback

Blogspot: Finding Publications in and out of Print

Items published through formal channels can be discontinued, although change is usually faster in information generated through informal channels.

For instance, is the book *Tartan Map of Scotland*, published by Harper Collins in 1999, still in print? Hint: Consider such resources as *Books in Print* to help you. Explain the steps you followed to find an answer to this question in your blog. Can you find this information via another pathway?

may not always move along linearly from stage to stage but may loop back. For example, although a manuscript has moved from the author to the publisher, editorial changes may be required, necessitating a loop back to the author for implementation. Time required at each stage is dependent upon the tasks to be completed at a particular stage. The whole process can take years. On the other hand, the publication process we have discussed here offers a formal chain of events that enables us to trace a work and consider the desirability of channeling information in this way. The key for us now is to understand how to use this knowledge to resolve daily information queries.

Using Our Understanding of the Formal Publication Process to Solve Information Problems

How can understanding the traditional, formal publication process help us solve everyday information problems? We can use our understanding of this process to help us locate particular information about various steps in the process or about the cycle as a whole. We may be faced with information problems and questions, including the following:

Information problem: I really enjoyed reading *The Brethren.* I've read all of John Grisham's previous books. Now I want to read another legal thriller by this author, if one has been published since that publication. *Information to locate:* The publication date of the *The Brethren* and John Grisham books published since then

Step 1: We know the name of the author whose works we wish to find. We also have identified the last Grisham novel we have read. To locate a novel published since *The Brethren,* we should now consider the publication date of this novel. This information can be found in several ways. Some obvious routes to this information include examining the verso (the page after the title page) in our copy of *The Brethren* or locating the title in our local library's online public-access catalogue (OPAC) to determine the date

(continued)

of publication. If we do this, we will find that *The Brethren* was published in 2000. With the year of publication in hand, we can search for John Grisham books published after 2000.

Step 2: Given our examination of the publication process, we know that the titles of forthcoming books and books currently in print are added to publishers' lists of titles and other databases of titles to announce the publication and to assist librarians, booksellers, and members of the public with selection and acquisition of publications. The wide dissemination of this information provides us with different paths we might take to information about publications.

We could use a library OPAC to search for titles by Grisham. However, the success of this search depends on whether or not the library you approach has acquired all of Grisham's titles published since 2000. This strategy may or may not retrieve a fully comprehensive list in response to your query. Remember that you can use the WorldCat's *Find in a Library* function in Google or Yahoo! search engines to locate book titles in collections.

We might also search for Grisham's official website, assuming that he has one. Locating this site, we find a list of his published works, in order of publication year. We can focus now on novels published since 2000 and we find the following titles posted on the site:

A Painted House, 2001
Skipping Christmas, 2001
The Summons, 2002
The King of Torts, 2003
Bleachers, 2003
The Last Juror, 2004
The Broker, 2005
The Innocent Man, 2006
The Appeal, 2008
The Associate: A Novel, 2009
Ford County: Stories, 2009

It is important to evaluate again the information we have accessed. If we decide that we want to find all of Grisham's titles published since 2000, then this list may satisfy us. However, if we want to find only the legal dramas that are similar to *The Brethren*, then we need to read about each book title carefully. For example, *The Innocent Man* is listed as Grisham's first nonfiction title. In addition, *A Painted House*, *Skipping Christmas*, and *Bleachers* are not the sorts of legal dramas we are looking for. We may wish to adjust our query accordingly.

A standard resource for tracking information about forthcoming and in/out-of-print publications is the *Books in Print* database. An author search for John Grisham should retrieve a comprehensive list of all of his works. We can further refine our search of this resource to retrieve only Grisham's legal fiction published after 2000. Interestingly, we will locate multilingual versions as well.

Although *Books in Print* is usually available by subscription, libraries and your local bookstore are likely to have access to this resource and may provide you with access as well. However, it has also become customary practice among a growing number of information searchers to turn to the freely and easily accessible online Amazon bookstore, as an alternative to *Books in Print*. Take care if you substitute this type of resource for a resource such as *Books in Print*. A search of Amazon will retrieve only those works on sale through that vendor, as opposed to a comprehensive list.

Information problem: I want to find a publisher who will publish my book. *Information to locate:* A list of publishing houses

Step 1: To find a publisher to publish a book we have authored, we need the names of publishing houses. In other words, we need to find a list of publishing houses. Immediately, we are thinking about information organized in list form. Key ideas here are *list* and *publisher*.

Step 2: Having ascertained the information that would most likely answer our query, our next step is to identify a source for this information. A directory of publishers would help us. Individual countries publish lists of publishers belonging to publishers' associations; for example, the National Library of Australia, www.nla.gov.au/libraries/resource/bookpub .html, maintains a comprehensive list of Australian booksellers and publishers who may be located online. There are also more wide-reaching resources; for example, Publishers' Catalogues, www.lights.com/publisher, provides links to publishers worldwide.

Step 3: We can select a directory and then proceed to examine the list of publishers to match our publishing interest with potential publishers of our work.

Locating this information can also provide other useful information. For instance, once we have selected a publishing house from our list, we can locate information about that particular publishing house, such as a genre of books or works targeted at a particular audience, such as children, that a particular publishing house produces.

Communities of Information Sharing

Different communities share information in particular ways. While social networking sites such as Facebook enable us all to contribute as we choose to developing relationships with others online, other communities, such as the scholarly community, have specific mechanisms for disseminating the information that emanates from its members. The key issue when considering communities of information sharing is trust. We need to be able to identify sources of information we trust and to understand why we trust these information sources. The speed of information exchange makes social networking sites, blogs, and wikis attractive alternatives to information dissemination. The traditional, formal channels employed by the scholarly community function more slowly, prompting some community members to take advantage of well-known and newer collaborative sharing approaches, including discussion lists and Facebook, to communicate, in addition to formal mechanisms of information exchange.

Communication in the Research Community

Research affects our daily lives. For example, a cure or treatment for an illness may change our lives or the life of someone we know. Reading a full or original research report may be preferable to reading a summary produced by the media. It is useful, therefore, to explore how the research community functions, to help us understand the types and forms of literature produced in the research process.

If we map the research process, we can isolate stages in the creation and distribution of new knowledge.

The author or researcher may be considered to be the beginning of the creative process, although the inspiration researchers take from the works of others informs the research work they undertake. The researcher determines the nature and design of a research project and implements this work. The academy and public and private funding sources help support research projects. The duration of the project depends on the nature of the investigation and may last for a very short time or for years.

Communication has always been a crucial element of research, permeating the entire research process. Although we may think of researchers as individuals working alone, they also work in groups and participate in social networks. For example, a researcher may form connections with researchers who share subject expertise. The networking of colleagues in the research process, classically called *invisible colleges*, underpins the progression of research and occurs at varying stages of the process.

Conferences have traditionally offered researchers the opportunity to meet in person with other researchers. In addition, a conference provides a forum for researchers to showcase their ongoing and completed work, as well as to share ideas with other researchers. The experience allows the other researchers to ask questions that, in turn, may inspire the speaker to reconsider or further develop the research as presented.

Although the conference itself may take place over a short period of a few days, participation in the conference requires forward planning, with submission of a paper to a conference board for peer review months in advance of the conference date, time allowed for the review process to occur, time allowed for revisions, and time allowed for possible resubmission and review, if required.

> *Research is formalized curiosity. It is poking and prying with a purpose.*
>
> —Zora Neale Hurston
> (1903–1960)

Research outputs through conferences may include the conference program, preconference prints of abstracts and/or papers, and final conference proceedings. These outputs may appear through mixed formal and informal channels. For example, conference proceedings may become part of the formal publication process discussed earlier. However, the conference program and preconference prints of abstracts and papers may be produced in a more temporary format that is not picked up in a similar publication. Instead, the conference program may appear on a website until the end of the conference or may be distributed at the conference in printed form.

Publication of a final research outcome may take the form of an article, book, report, or other manifestation of the researcher's work. For researchers, formal channels of publication form an essential outcome of a research project that broadcasts the research results and helps to justify funding for this project as well as future funding for projects. The "publish or perish" phenomenon accentuates the need to put work in the public domain, again demanding of researchers and academics that they justify their positions through contributions to the formal body of literature in a given field.

Peer review or *refereeing* is the research community's method of evaluating and maintaining high quality of standards in publications. Experts in a subject field review research outputs, and their informed opinions form the basis for acceptance or rejection of a manuscript for publication. Peer-reviewed publications are highly desirable in the research community, since the peer-review process denotes reliability and credibility in published works. Although the process is not infallible, occasionally failing to expose counterfeit research, and extends time to publication by months, peer review remains the main means of formal community evaluation of research.

Using Our Understanding of the Research Process to Locate Published Works

Understanding the research process can assist us with decision making as we search for and select information. The research process highlights different types of information available at different stages of the process and through which channels we can expect to receive and to locate this information.

We may be interested only in the final outputs of a research project, leading us to search the body of literature, often peer reviewed, resulting from ongoing publishing of research findings. For example, we can search indexes for research articles in academic journals.

Locating literature that does not come under bibliographic control exercised over formally published research works can pose a greater challenge. Works such as interim research reports, conference papers, and preprints or items produced in advance of formal publication, pamphlets, company reports, and internal organizational communications all fall under the heading of informal information communication and may be all much more difficult to trace. In some cases, these sorts of informal communications may become formal communications through publication at a later stage; on the other hand, some of this material never reaches the public domain, meaning that we could be missing valuable, comprehensive, up-to-date information about research projects. Certainly the exchanges between researchers navigating the research process would remain hidden to us, unless individuals or groups make public announcements about their work. Research funding and project announcements may be posted on electronic mailing lists, in bulletins, and in journal literature to ensure the information has a public presence, although this information is not necessarily collected and managed in a single location. The difficulty with materials escaping formal channels of bibliographic control adds to a body of ephemeral or "gray" literature.

The challenge of gray literature connected to the research process is not, however, insurmountable. We acquire items every day outside the formal channels of communication we have discussed. One means of resolving our dilemma with locating and relocating information that is "here today and gone tomorrow" is to save gray literature—for instance, in print or even via bookmarks in a web browser—and build a collection of gray literature of our own. Librarians have long used this technique to satisfy questions posed by library patrons.

Collections of gray literature are essential to overcoming the temporal and often disposable nature of this type of information, such as posters and handouts that are often discarded after use. Companies and organizations may also maintain collections of the gray literature they produce—pamphlets, brochures, marketing reports, and similar efforts. Educational and government institutions may also gather and organize gray literature. Collections of gray literature may be research-area specific; for example, arXiv, located at http://lanl.arXiv.org or http://xxx.lanl.gov, provides open Internet access to e-prints in the subject areas of physics, mathematics, computer science, and quantitative biology.

Initiatives and news about gathering and organizing gray literature across a variety of subject areas may be found through GreyNet, formally known as the Grey Literature Network Service, www.greynet.org. This service promotes collection of, as well as research and communication about, gray literature. In addition to codifying and highlighting gray literature via its website, GreyNet maintains a public presence through conference participation and the production of the *Grey Journal*, an international journal about the issues surrounding gray literature, including its collection and use.

Communication in Our Everyday Lives

Information permeates every aspect of our daily lives. We share that information with one another through a variety of formal and informal channels that go beyond the mechanisms of communication discussed so far. The means by which we receive information and the nature of the source of information determine our trust of the information overall.

Often our relationship with the provider of the information can increase our trust of the information; in other words, we trust the source and, therefore, we trust the information received from that source, even though the information delivered may be inaccurate or incomplete. For example, a common misconception with regard to information delivery is, "The computer says so, and it is always correct." It is essential that we remain vigilant about the quality of the information we receive, even when we approach information published through formal channels.

Informal communities of sharing, whether people you know in your neighborhood or people connecting with each other online, are often useful as a means of spreading a message quickly. Blogs, as we have discussed in this textbook, have increased dramatically in popularity as a means of sending a message into the public domain. Blogs have attained such a following that some businesses are incorporating the idea of corporate blogs into their communications options. Others prefer networks of information sharing in which they choose to add a range of visual messages, vacation films, anecdotal ramblings, music videos, and so forth to websites such as YouTube, www.youtube.com, which provides a ready forum for this

Blogspot: Learning through Social Groups

As we know, social networking sites are popular places for people to meet and join together through groups. Using a social networking site, such as Facebook, locate a group devoted to the yeast extract called Marmite. What information does this group provide?

Now, using published journal literature, locate research involving Marmite.

Compare and contrast the information you have located. What is the value of each approach to exploring the world of Marmite?

information and also tracks popularity of items posted. Still others share information through social networking sites, such as Facebook, www.face book.com, or MySpace, www.myspace.com, using the sites to post textual as well as visual information, to join groups focused on common interests, and to stay in touch with as well as meet new contacts. In some cases, such as the 2009 election in Iran, a combination of Twitter, www.twitter.com, and mobile technology offered a means for individuals to communicate about the election results with the wider world when the official press was unable to do so.

Using Everyday Information Communities to Help Us Locate Information

Information communities exist all around us, ranging from people connecting in the short term to achieve a particular goal to people developing long-term relationships. For example, we are bombarded with health information every day through news reports, advertisements, health care providers and services, and so on. We can identify different groups that have a stake in the overall provision of health services information, and then identify and evaluate which formal and informal channels and sources we would trust to solve a particular health information problem.

Information Problem: I have heard that high levels of cortisol are unhealthy and may be a precursor to diabetes.
Information to Locate: What is a healthy level of cortisol? Are high levels of cortisol related to diabetes?

In addition to developing an overall plan to solve this information problem, we should pay special attention here to the nature of the sources and channels of information we will trust.

Several pathways are open to us as we investigate this question. Remember to brainstorm possible means of solving your problem. What pathways to the required information are available to you? For example, you might choose to search formal information sources, such as peer-reviewed,

(*continued*)

published medical research articles on the topic as found in health information databases, like *Medline* or *Cinahl*. You might also consult a health professional, such as a doctor, nurse, or dietician. Alternatively, you might investigate more informal pathways to information about cortisol, such as an Internet search, potentially producing such informal sources as a discussion list or blog, through which people with relevant health issues share their experiences, and private web pages devoted to the topic, as well as formal sources that have been posted on the Internet, such as medical reports. You might also find gray literature, such as pamphlets and brochures produced by a medical clinic, government institution, or health-related business that provides useful information. In each case, you need to evaluate the authority and reliability of each source of information and then decide how each piece of information found helps fill the gaps in your understanding.

Exercise

1. (a) What is an ISBN? What is the ISBN for Bill Levinson's *In the Company of Wild Butterflies: An Intimate Study of the Secret Lives of Wild Butterflies?*
   (b) What is an ISSN? What is the ISSN for the *Japanese Journal of Applied Entomology and Zoology?*
2. Build a collection of links to electronic gray literature on the topic of *homeopathic health care for cancer patients*, using the bookmarking function in your web browser.

Information Hunt

1. Find a list of publishers of children's stories.
2. What is the latest book on fashion available by authors Trinny Woodall and Susannah Constantine?
3. Who published *Ethics of Spying: A Reader for the Intelligence Professional?*
4. Using WorldCat, locate the Singapore library that holds Andy Wibbels' *BlogWild! A Guide for Small Business Blogging* in its collection.

5. Find reports on the use of Psyllium to reduce LDL cholesterol, using both formal and informal information channels.
6. Find three different publishers' catalogues for sociology texts.
7. Use Google's *Product Search* to locate catalogues of comics.
8. Find a collection of movie posters. How would you categorize this type of information?
9. What publications, if any, were issued after the two-day seminar *Promoting Occupational Safety and Health Research in the EU*?
10. Is the student journal *The Journal of Young Investigators* a peer-reviewed publication?

CHAPTER 7

Researching for Writing

Researching and writing an academic paper require particular skills that provide the foundation for a successful education. However, many of these skills are also transferable to other areas of everyday information seeking and use. Regardless of whether you are writing your first essay, preparing a research project, or even writing for the popular press, developing the skills needed to effectively navigate, select, and synthesize research literature will strengthen your confidence and ability to tackle this task.

> *Is the world ending? I have to research a paper on Bosnia for tomorrow, but if the world's ending, I'm not gonna bother.*
>
> —Cordelia, *Buffy the Vampire Slayer*, "Helpless," Season 3, Episode 12, 1997

What You Will Learn in This Chapter

In this chapter, we focus on building pathways through and means of exploring and keeping up to date with different literatures. By understanding how various literature, such as journals and newspapers, is organized and made accessible, you will be better prepared to extract the information relevant to your information need. In this chapter, you will learn to do the following:

- Map the process of finding and evaluating information onto the stages of paper preparation

- Use a range of indexes effectively to locate periodical literature
- Consider ways of information monitoring with personalized news alerts
- Locate a published review
- Build an annotated reference list

The Writing Process

At one time or another, we all find ourselves in a situation where we need to write a piece, whether a letter to a newspaper, a report for work, or an essay for a course. In each instance, information plays a critical role, informing different parts of the process. As you approach a writing task, consider the stages of this process. Developing an effective plan to navigate the process at this point will help you make more efficient use of your time.

You will be writing on a particular topic. Narrow the topic as much as possible. If you are uncertain about the topic area or if it is new to you, this is a good time to do a little exploratory reading. Remember that factual information resources, such as encyclopedias, can help you here. The topic must be manageable in the context of the piece of writing you will do. For instance, suppose you plan to write a piece about building a house. You might narrow your topic focus to house designs. However, this revised topic is still fairly broad. You might select one aspect of house design, such as interior design. You can still narrow your topic further. You might narrow interior design to focus on one room, such as the bathroom, and from there select one aspect of bathroom design, such as bathtubs, and then consider styles, manufacturers, and functions of bathtubs as possible avenues of exploration. Then you might decide to examine one particular type of bathtub, such as the Jacuzzi.

From this narrowed focus, you should develop a thesis statement or proposition, that is, a single statement that expresses what you will consider in your writing. Invest some time in this step. The proposition you devise will guide the development of your project, including your information seeking. Think here about a burning question you might have about your topic. Now convert this question into a statement, taking care to make this statement as specific as you can. Using our bathtub example, we might create a thesis statement: Jacuzzi bathtubs offer significant health benefits. Although you may feel that a pointed statement will not allow enough scope for the length of the piece you are writing, keep refining your proposition as much as you can. A specific thesis statement will actually streamline your project, enabling you to sift through information with greater ease and speed. Write your proposition on a piece of paper and keep it somewhere in plain view to remind you of your purpose in this writing project. Remember that you can modify this statement as necessary as your work continues.

The next step is often called a review of the literature. This is a point at which your developing information skills will come to the fore. Remember to build a search strategy. In addition, we discuss in this chapter some of the finer points of the information hunting you will need to do to locate materials for your literature review, specifically examining the role of indexes in mining periodically published literature.

Once you have located materials, read strategically and critically. You have several important decisions to make about the information you have found. Once you have identified a list of potentially useful items, you need to sift through this information and select those pieces with greatest value to your project. Be sure to examine bibliographic details, abstracts, and introductions carefully to help you evaluate the potential usefulness and appropriateness of a given work to your project. Take notes to remind yourself of your reasons for selecting a particular item for inclusion in your literature review. Note taking can be accomplished in a number of ways. In addition to traditional jotting of notes on the front of an article or on a notepad, you can take notes electronically, via a laptop, tablet personal computer, or even a handheld device with capacity to download information to another computer. You may find that your library provides an electronic facility for searching and then capturing bibliographic details of retrieved items, with the option to add notes of your own.

When you read the item in full, be sure again to read it critically, taking descriptive as well as evaluative notes about the content of the work and its relevance to points you wish to make in your own piece. Question what you read and consider whether or not the author has provided sufficient evidence to convince you of his or her argument.

Use your notes to sketch an outline for your work. Include as much detail as possible, such as your thesis statement, your main points organized logically so that each progresses naturally from the previous point, and subpoints and examples to illustrate your points. Your outline will map your strategy for writing.

As you write, keep your audience in mind. Readers will evaluate your work critically. This is your opportunity to convince them of the value of your argument and your work. Authors take different approaches to writing. If you are writing a short piece, it may be feasible to write a draft in one sitting; however, longer pieces can be ongoing for days and weeks. In this latter situation, try to write smaller segments in one sitting and write every day. The hardest part of writing is getting something on that blank page. Writing continuously will help keep writer's block at bay and will help you feel confident about accomplishing even part of your draft. Once you have completed a draft, set it aside for a day or two. Then return to it and read what you have written critically for style, content, logic, and cohesion. Many students ignore this step; it is one of the most common reasons for failing to improve in writing. Revise until you are satisfied that your work meets the highest possible standard.

Throughout this process, try to keep track of the bibliographic references for the works you select, read, and refer to in your own work. To help you, we discuss building a reference list later in this chapter. And finally, remember to manage your time. Always allow sufficient time to do the thinking, researching, writing, and revising appropriate to the project at hand.

Quick Tips: Planning and Completing a Piece of Writing

To make the most of the writing process, have you done the following?

- Narrowed your topic as much as possible?
- Developed a one-line, specific thesis statement or proposition?
- Identified and selected literature to support your thesis statement?
- Read critically the literature you have gathered?
- Outlined your paper?
- Written your work, keeping your audience in mind?
- Revised your work?
- Given credit to those whose work you have used in your writing?

Common Tasks in Researching for Writing

FINDING A REVIEW

A review is an evaluation of an item, including fiction and nonfiction books, reference tools, electronic databases, film, music, and so forth, published in a variety of venues, such as journals, newspapers, and the Internet. Locating a review is an essential skill for students, who may use reviews to gauge the potential usefulness of an item to their own work. Students are often asked to locate a review of a particular work and then to write a review of their own. However, knowing how to find a review can be a useful skill for us all. We can use reviews to help us make decisions about an item—for instance, to evaluate whether to read or possibly purchase a particular book. A software review can help us compare the functionality of two similar pieces of software and select one application for our use. In both instances, the ability to locate a review of an item can help us make everyday decisions.

The challenge in finding a review is twofold. First, we need to consider the nature of the information we hope to find. Will any review suffice, or do we require a particular sort of review, such as a review written by an individual with special qualifications enabling him or her to make an assessment of an item? Second, we need to understand how reviews are organized. Once we understand the structure of this type of literature, we can establish a path to guide us to the review we want to find.

Google Books and WorldCat both provide access to reviews of publications. For instance, a search of either resource for *One Good Turn* by Kate Atkinson returns not only the bibliographic details for this book but also brief reviews written by readers within the application and in external applications, such as Amazon's online bookshop and WeRead.com (also available through Facebook). Google Books further provides links to reviews published in newspapers and other resources on the Internet. Although both Google Books and WorldCat enable us to view the rankings and reviews written by other readers, remember that the authority of these reviews may not be so easily discernable. Publishers of reviews, such as the *New York Times'* Books section, www.nytimes.com/pages/books, are established, authoritative entities that have become trusted sources for reviews.

The published review literature is often organized through indexes, although exceptions exist. Reviews are often identified either within databases documenting content of journals and magazines, or as collections with dedicated indexes. For example, AcqWeb's Directory of Book Reviews on the Web, http://acqweb.org/bookrev.html, is maintained by acquisitions librarians to provide links to various international review sites for a variety of media. Books and Book Reviews on the Web, http://home.mchsi.com/~albeej/pages/Books.html, offers links to book review and book sites, as well as help for locating books, bibliographies, and other materials for different subject areas. The *New York Review of Books*, www.nybooks.com/archives, provides an easily searchable archive of its published book reviews.

Various sources also cover reviews of different forms of media. For example, Search Engine Showdown Reviews, www.searchengineshowdown.com/reviews, evaluates Internet search engines and provides news of changes to search engines, such as those that become defunct. SuperKids Educational Software Review, www.superkids.com, offers reviews of educational software written by teachers, parents, and children in the United States. The well-known Internet Movie Database, www.imdb.com, provides a directory of film and television information, including published reviews, as well as reviews by the general public. For example, IMDB links *Beloved*, a 1998 movie based on Toni Morrison's book and starring Oprah Winfrey, to a list of reviews of the film, including one written by Roger Ebert, published in the *Chicago Sun-Times* on October 16, 1998.

The process of locating a review is outlined below. Remember, no single review index or collection will contain every review published. You may need to explore indexes and collections before you find those that are relevant to your search.

Information Problem: I want to know if I might like to read *Florence Nightingale: Avenging Angel* by Hugh Small.

Information to Locate: A review of a particular work to help me make a decision to read or not read the book

Step 1: Before we begin searching, it is important to assess what information we have and what information we need to proceed. In this case, we have the title of a book and the name of the author. Our pathway to a review will also influence the information we require for this search.

For instance, to pursue a review through printed indexes, we need to consider the particular organization of indexes in this format. Because printed book review indexes are generally published annually, we need to identify the year in which the book was published. We can establish the year of publication by consulting a resource such as *Books in Print*. Alternatively, if your library has your book in its collection, you can locate the year of publication using your library's OPAC or WorldCat to find the catalogue record for this item. You may also have the book in hand, in which case the year of publication will appear on the title page or verso in the book. Using one of these methods, we can find the publication year, 1998.

Step 2: Now we can consult an index. Again, the format of the index we select will shape our pathway to a review.

For example, we might choose *Book Review Digest* in print form. This index is published annually, which may, at first glance, make our search appear daunting. However, we know that our book was published in 1998, so we can logically assume that reviews of our book will appear approximately as the book was published or after publication. Scanning entries, listed alphabetically by author's surname, in our case "Small, Hugh. *Florence Nightingale: Avenging Angel*," three references to reviews of our book are found in the 2001 volume of *Book Review Digest*, as follows:

Booklist, v. 98 no. 5, p. 496, 1999, William Beatty
Library Journal, v. 124 no. 15, p. 92, 1999, David Keymer
NY Review Books, v. 48 no. 24, p. 16–19, 2001, Helen Epstein

To locate a review using an electronic database, we might choose Swetswise. Using the advanced search option, we can enter the search string *"Florence Nightingale: Avenging Angel" AND review* to search for a review of our book.

Step 3: Next, we must find or view our review.

If we have followed a route through printed indexes, then we must now locate the review specified in the index reference. We can search our library's OPAC for the name of the journal in which the review has been published, for example, *New York Review of Books*, locate volume 48, issue 24 of that journal on the shelf in the library, and find the review on page 16, as outlined in the index reference.

An electronic database will yield either a reference to a review or the full text of the review. Our Swetswise search leads us to the full text of a review, which we need only read on screen or print it out. However, had we found only a reference to a review in an electronic database, we would again need to search our library's OPAC for the relevant journal, as outlined above.

Quick Tips: Finding a Review Using Indexes and Collections of Reviews

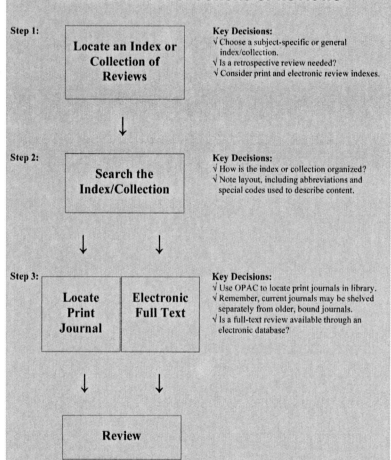

Step 1:

Locate an Index or Collection of Reviews

Key Decisions:
√ Choose a subject-specific or general index/collection.
√ Is a retrospective review needed?
√ Consider print and electronic review indexes.

Step 2:

Search the Index/Collection

Key Decisions:
√ How is the index or collection organized?
√ Note layout, including abbreviations and special codes used to describe content.

Step 3:

Locate Print Journal

Electronic Full Text

Key Decisions:
√ Use OPAC to locate print journals in library.
√ Remember, current journals may be shelved separately from older, bound journals.
√ Is a full-text review available through an electronic database?

Review

TRACING CITATIONS

Varying types of indexes serve various purposes. In addition to providing a pointing system to items within a subject literature, indexes can serve wider purposes. For example, a citation index can be used to track citation patterns in a body of literature. Tracking items cited by an author can help you locate further items of relevance to your own research. A citation index can also help to identify potentially critical studies in a subject area retrospectively, given the number of times a work has been cited by other authors. Citation indexes exist for diverse subject areas—for example, *Sciences Citation Index*, *Arts & Humanities Citation Index*, and *Social Sciences Citation Index*—and all are searchable through the Web of Science database.

Citation indexes can also help you to trace second authors, as well as the works cited in an item's bibliography. Although the use of a citation index can assist our information searching, citation indexes are also sometimes used to help measure an author's publication record. This method of assessing output can be contentious, for example, if an author more frequently appears as a third or subsequent author of a work, as opposed to first or second author, and the citation index does not pick up third or successive contributors to a piece. For this reason, we should never assume that we have located a complete picture of an author's publications through a citation index. With that caveat, however, citation indexes can be very helpful for exploring patterns of publication in a subject area. Suppose we wanted to discover the number of times a particular work has been cited.

Information Problem: How many times has H. J. Brightman's 1981 article "Constraints to Effective Problem-solving," published in *Business*, volume 31, issue 2, been cited?
Information to Locate: Number of citations of this article

Step 1: As always, consider what information you have at hand. In this case, we have nearly complete citation details for the article in question. We can use a citation index to locate the article and relevant citation information provided for this article.
Step 2: Using the Web of Science, we can conduct a Cited Reference Search to locate the article. For example, we can search by author, entering Brightman, H* or Brightman, HJ into the search box.

(continued)

> *Step 3:* From the results list of works by that author's name, we can identify the relevant article. For example, we can align our known publication date, 1981, with those provided in the results list. Alternatively, we can select Show Expanded Titles to see a full list of title information, including article titles where possible.
>
> *Step 4:* Either approach narrows our list to one possible record, for which we can select View Record to see full citation information about this work.
>
> *Step 5:* Under Times Cited, we can see that Brightman's article has been cited twice. We can then view the articles citing Brightman and cited by Brightman, both as textual citations and as graphical representations of citing patterns.

SEARCHING THE POPULAR PRESS

Individual newspapers and news services provide direct access to their stories. For instance, the *New York Times*, www.nytimes.com, features searchable indexes, as well as keyword searching, of current and archived news hosted through the database vendor ProQuest. The BBC, or British Broadcasting Corporation, provides a comprehensive news site, www.bbc.co.uk, where you can read 24-hour news stories, watch news videos, and gather information about special topics, as well as link to other BBC sections, such as entertainment. Although we may often turn to a favorite news source, it is also possible to search collections of newspapers and news stories gathered through a number of services.

To begin, different resources gather information about news sources to help us identify one or more news sources relevant to our problem solving. *Ulrich's Periodicals Directory*, which we reviewed in chapter 5, supplies information about periodically published literature worldwide, including newspapers. In addition, a number of databases are dedicated to documenting newspapers. For instance, the LexisNexis (News & Business) database covers full-text searching of newspapers from around the world and in multiple languages, including such well-known titles as the *New York Times*, the *Times* and *Sunday Times*, and the *Financial Times*. *Keesing's World News Archive*, www.keesings.com, offers summaries of news stories from around the world, dating from 1931 to the present. *Keesing's* provides keyword searching, enhanced by date limitation and sorting by relevance and date options. To help you keep abreast of topics

Blogspot: Exploring Newspapers

Although newspapers vary in overall presentation, there are still similarities in content included and how content is organized. Select two printed newspapers and two online newspapers. Compare and contrast newspapers, noting for each:

* What information is included in each newspaper?
* How is information organized in the newspaper?
* What tools or devices (e.g., indexes, lists of contents, headlines) are provided to help you navigate the newspaper?
* How does format (paper v. electronic) affect organization of information?

Discuss your observations in your blog.

of current interest, you can also select from clouds of terms assigned to represent article content, as well as clusters of references about a topic, with tags generated by *Keesing's* and the general public.

Chipwrapper, www.chipwrapper.co.uk (named for the traditional vendor wrapping of fish and chips in newspaper in Britain), provides searching of U.K. newspaper content published online. Online Newspapers, www.onlinenewspapers.com, offers one-stop searching of newspapers around the world, with searches by individual countries or all countries possible. Various Internet search engines further collect news stories from different news feeds, such as Google News and Yahoo! News.

Staying on Top of the Latest News

Sometimes it's important to keep abreast of the latest developments in an area. One way of monitoring what is happening around us is to keep in touch with the news. There are many ways of tracking news stories. RSS or Really Simple Syndication offers a convenient method of bringing news to our desktop.

What is an RSS or Really Simple Syndication feed? Essentially, this is a form of news feed that you can direct to your computer. Using RSS feeds can assist us with our information monitoring, providing up-to-the-moment information as stories become available. Think of RSS as news that comes conveniently to you through your computer, enabling you to read stories as they become available on news sites.

Information Problem: I would like current news stories delivered to my computer desktop.

Information to Locate: Continuous RSS feed set up on my computer desktop

Step 1: We can use an aggregator program or a news reader to customize ongoing news delivery to our computer. This form of software can be freely downloaded from the Internet. A typical news reader is Awasu, available for download at www.awasu.com. Awasu helpfully provides a tour that explains software features, including setting channels, selecting alert mechanisms for breaking news stories, archiving stories already received, and extracting information from news stories. We need only visit the Awasu homepage and download a personal edition of the software.

Step 2: Using our Awasu browser, we can add some news feeds to the list we wish to monitor. For example, we can add the URLs for Google News and BBC News to our list.

Step 3: We can then select Update to view the latest news provided through our selected news feeds in our Awasu browser.

Blogspot: Adding RSS to Our Blog

An alternative way of keeping up with news is to add an RSS feed to our blog.

1. Open your blog at www.blogger.com.
2. Select *Customize.*
3. Select *Add a Page Element* at the bottom of the page. A list of options will appear in a new window.
4. Scroll down to *Feed—Add content from an RSS or Atom feed to your blog.*
5. Select the *Add to Blog* button for this option.
6. Copy and paste an RSS URL of your choice to the box provided. For example, try adding the BBC's RSS feed, http://news.bbc.co.uk/1/hi/help/rss/3223484.stm.
7. Select the *Continue* button.
8. Select *Save Changes* button.
9. View your blog to see the change you have made.

Now find an RSS feed of your choice and add it to your blog.

Building a Reference List

As you identify and select items to use in your paper or report, bear in mind that you will need to provide a bibliography or reference list of those items you have drawn upon for information. Always take note of the full bibliographic details for the sources you consult as you search for and locate information, connecting sources to the notes you take as you read. It is essential that you keep track of information and sources that influence your work. In addition, try to paraphrase, or describe in your own words, the points you consider worthwhile noting. Remember that using material in either quoted or paraphrased text without giving credit to the creator of that work is considered plagiarism or theft, the penalty for which can range from censure or expulsion from an academic program to lawsuits for compensation.

You can compile bibliographic information on an ongoing basis by simply keeping track of your sources on paper; however, bibliographic software programs such as *Endnote*, *RefWorks*, and *Library Master* offer a powerful means of managing this information. You may also wish to create your own means of information management, utilizing a spreadsheet or word-processing program to adapt the information management tool to your individual needs. Bibliographic software programs enable you to build your own catalogue of sources from which you can select particular items to include in the reference list for a given paper and cite sources within your paper. The software will automatically format your reference list and your citations in the bibliographic style of your choice.

Creating lists of works is also easily done through WorldCat and Google Books. In each case, we can create our own library of works, essentially gathering together content we choose in one area. For example, if we search Google Books for *The Outlaws of Medieval Legend* by Maurice H. Keen, we can find bibliographic details for this item, along with a picture of the book cover. By selecting *Add to My Library*, we can add this item to our list. We can also export our library to our computer by selecting *Export My Library* and then the *Save File* option in our account area in Google Books. WorldCat enables us to locate the same monograph and add it to a list we create within WorldCat. Once we have created our list of materials, we can select a citation style (e.g., Harvard, MLA, APA) and export our lists as bibliographies for use in Microsoft Excel and our Endnote and RefWorks applications. When exporting your list, the appropriate software application (e.g., Endnote) will automatically launch on your computer, enabling you to add the items on your list directly into your current reference list on your computer. WorldCat provides step-by-step instructions via video (e.g., www.youtube.com/watch?v=X8W7kWMrVNk), available through WorldCat and YouTube, to assist you with creating reference lists. For convenience, WorldCat is accessible through Facebook, providing access to WorldCat's list functions. Both bibliographic software packages and Internet applications such as Google Books and WorldCat allow the addition of notes and searchable keywords to the individual works on our list. Although you can add large amounts of text to a record, a simple way to keep track of the content of the sources you consult is a brief annotation. Your annotations can then be combined with the bibliographic data for works to generate an annotated bibliography, that is, a bibliography providing annotations with entries.

An annotation summarizes the major elements of a given work. Depending on the purpose of the annotation, it may include a brief description of content as well as evaluative notes. Although length may approach about 150 words, annotations are often only a couple of lines of text. The purpose of your annotation will determine the length of what you write. Aim for a concise but informative summary.

Practice writing annotations for the items you have stored in Endnote or RefWorks, whether the item is an article, book, or some other form of information.

Quick Tips: Writing Annotations

An annotation is a concise, often evaluative summary of a book, article, or other item. When writing an annotation, remember to address the following questions as appropriate in the annotation:

- What is the purpose of the annotation—descriptive, evaluative, or both?
- What are the qualifications (subject knowledge) of the work's author?
- What is the author's viewpoint?
- What is the purpose of the work?
- What are the main points of the work?
- How does this item relate to other works on the subject?
- Who is the audience for the work?

—ww—

Exercise

1. Why is RSS useful in finding information? Set up a news alert in your news reader by adding channels to update you on the subject area of your choice.
2. Find ten works on the topic of managing corporate image. Enter these into a bibliographic software package of your choice (e.g., RefWorks, Endnote). Include an annotation for each work. Use the software and your collected publications to generate an annotated bibliography. Can you create a similar reference list using WorldCat lists?

Information Hunt

Locate reviews of the following items:

1. David Bainbridge's book *The X in Sex: How the X Chromosome Controls Our Lives*
2. U2's *How to Dismantle an Atomic Bomb*, music CD
3. Douglas Adam's *The Hitchhiker's Guide to the Universe*, book, TV series, and movie
4. *Nancy Drew: Deception on Danger Island*, interactive software
5. WiseNut search engine
6. Philip N. Howard and Steve Jones' book, *Society Online: The Internet in Context*
7. Irris Makler's book *Our Woman in Kabul*
8. *The Incredibles* movie
9. Margaret Atwood's book *The Blind Assassin*
10. Thelonious Monk with John Coltrane, music CD

CHAPTER 8

Counting on Our Numeric Literacy

Working with numbers is as important as being able to move with ease through textual information. To be able to solve routine daily problems and make decisions, we need to be comfortable with numbers, graphs, and symbols. Understanding how to find, interpret, and evaluate numeric information can help us finesse a problem and build a strong argument through evidence. From counting to measuring, understanding patterns, and organizing and managing numeric information, we rely upon our numeracy skills, or our quantitative literacy, to help us with ordinary functions every day.

Numeric information is gathered, organized, and disseminated just as we've seen for other forms of information. Presented as raw data or interpreted in relation to other numeric data, this information is often used as evidence to support a point of view. Understanding how numeric data can be massaged and packaged is essential to deciding how to interpret and use a seemingly complicated part of our information world effectively.

What You Will Learn in This Chapter

In this chapter, our focus is numeric information to help you learn to do the following:

- Identify numeric information in its various forms
- Understand means of organizing numeric information

- Locate numeric information
- Consider interpretative issues with numeric information
- Evaluate numeric information for decision making

Making Numbers Count

What do we mean by numeric information? How can numeric information assist us in our information worlds? Understanding the nature of numeric information is the first step in our journey to numeric literacy.

Numeric information includes all information related to numbers. This can range from raw numeric data, such as the number of members in a club, to statistical summations of numeric data, such as comparisons of corporate earnings by product between different quarterly periods. Basically, if you can count or measure something, you have numeric data. Once numeric data is placed in context, this becomes numeric information.

> *Numbers are the product of counting. Quantities are the product of measurement.*
>
> —Gregory Bateson
> (1904–1980)

The Organization of Numeric Information

We see numeric information all around us every day, in advertising, news reports, and so forth. In private enterprise, companies and individuals present numeric information about finances, production, markets, and other related topics. Similarly, public or government bodies at national and local levels publish numeric information related to all aspects of our daily lives, including census data and statistical compilations, vital statistics, crime reports, agricultural production, disease pandemics, energy and resources, and politics. Name an area of interest to you and you will find that someone has compiled and published numeric information about this subject.

Some groups are devoted to publishing only numeric information. For example, government bodies such as Statistics Canada exist to provide numeric information to the public, in this case numeric information about all aspects of life in Canada—its population, resources, economy, society, and culture—to enable individuals and groups to make decisions about policies, strategies, and programs. To that end, Statistics Canada publishes a mixture of free and payment-required publications, such as reports, study results, and data. For example, *Community Profiles* from the 2006 Canadian Census, providing population demographics for small geographic areas online, and *Passing on the Ancestral Language,* an article about social trends in the preservation of languages in Canada, are Statistics Canada publications. Like many other organizations, Statistics Canada maintains a collection of its publications, printed publications in its own library collection, and many reports published in an online collection available for downloading through its website at www.statcan.ca. Depository libraries also collect Statistics Canada's publications, and these institutions can help you locate a publication not accessible online.

Within individual publications, numeric information may be organized in a variety of ways. Discrete pieces of numeric information may be represented as raw data, percentages, or as part of statistical analyses. Tabular presentation of numeric data allows for easy scanning of categories of information. Although the tabular format is common and is easily captured online for use in a spreadsheet, be prepared to find numeric information presented textually and graphically as well. For example, the United Nations' Economic and Social Commission for Asia and the Pacific annually publishes the *Statistical Yearbook for Asia and the Pacific.* Available for download via the Internet, this publication combines tabular data about specific topics, such as Child Health, comparing regions and time periods, as well as graphical representations of data and textual analysis. The World Health Organization (WHO) provides data and statistics on a variety of social topics in interactive formats via the Internet; for example, their Global Health Atlas can be used to generate a geographic representation of one or more countries and then add layers of information to that map, including demographic and socioeconomic indicators—population density, for example—as well as elements of infrastructure, such as settlement, health services, education services, natural features, and water services. Go to www.who.int/globalatlas and experiment with layering your own map.

Finding Numeric Information

Although numeric information continues to be published and disseminated in printed format, this type of information is increasingly disseminated through the Internet. Organization of this material can still bear the hallmarks of traditional bibliographic tools, including catalogues and bibliographies, so it is helpful to consult this sort of information tool. In addition, some of the factual information resources we discussed earlier, such as yearbooks, will also come in handy, particularly when looking for statistics for a particular country—Denmark's *Statistical Yearbook*, www.dst.dk/Yearbook.aspx, for example, or a subject area, such as the International Monetary Fund's *Government Finance Statistics Yearbook*.

The easiest way to locate numeric information is to consider who would compile and publish the material you need. Since governments, especially the U.S. government, produce a vast amount of publically available numeric information, you might begin by considering the agency that would publish the information you need or want. Remember to explore levels of governments from nation-specific to umbrella government bodies, such as the European Union and the United Nations. Understanding the organization of government is essential to identifying the government body relevant to your information query.

For example, if you wanted to register for a United Kingdom vehicle license, where would you begin? The registration of a vehicle in any country is most likely to be part of the remit of a transportation agency or department. In the United Kingdom, the government has a branch dedicated to transportation issues, the Department for Transport, which has as an executive agency, the Driver and Vehicle Licensing Agency (DVLA). The DVLA operates an official agency website, www.dvla.gov.uk, to provide information to the public about issues concerning drivers' licenses and vehicle registration.

Several resources also offer compilations of numeric data and information from wide-ranging sources. For example, the U.S. Central Intelligence Agency (CIA)'s *World Fact Book*, https://www.cia.gov/library/publications/the-world-factbook/index.html, is renowned for its coverage of information about countries around the world, including such topics as geographic boundaries, people, government, economy, communications, transportation, military, and transnational issues. For instance, under the country profile for Akrotiri, you can learn that this country is located on the southwest coast of Cyprus at geographic coordinates 34°37' N, 32°58' E, covers 123 square kilometers, has 56.3 kilometers of coastline, and has a population of approximately 15,700 people. Numeric information pervades the social information we learn in this source.

NUMERIC INFORMATION BY GEOGRAPHIC REGION

Searching for information by country or region is also useful. In 2006, Google released its U.S. Government Search, www.google.com/ig/usgov, formerly Google Uncle Sam. A similar resource is USA.gov, www.usa.gov, developed by the U.S. government to present information on various topics about United States. Yahoo! further maintains a section covering links to agencies providing government statistics in a number of countries.

The United States' FedStats, www.fedstats.gov, is another common source of an array of numeric information, providing access to statistical information searchable by various means, including state, subject, and comparative statistics internationally and within the United States. A search for crime statistics reveals links to several government agencies, including the Federal Bureau of Investigation (FBI), the Bureau of Prisons, the Drug Enforcement Administration (DEA), and the Bureau of Justice Statistics. A search by state produces data sets for information on population demographics, economics, and geographic spread, comparing data for a given state to national totals.

The *Statistical Abstract of the United States*, www.census.gov/com pendia/statab, published annually since 1878, draws on data gathered by various government and private organizations to provide one of the major sources of social, economic, and political statistics for that country. Highly specific numeric information gathered in this source can be searched using an online search facility or located through an online subject index. For example, a search for students carrying weapons reveals a summary table of numeric data gathered from the U.S. National Center for Education Statistics and the U.S. Bureau of Justice Statistics, www.census.gov/compen dia/statab/tables/08s0237.xls. Figures compare student reports of carrying weapons by gender, secondary school year, ethnicity, and year between 1993 and 2005. This numeric information has further potential value in comparing similar situations in other countries.

NUMERIC INFORMATION BY SUBJECT

We can also consider numeric information for a particular subject area. For example, health statistics are commonly sought, and a number of dedicated sources provide health-related numeric information related to this topic, and frequently now through the Internet. Offered through the U.S. National Library of Medicine and National Institutes of Health, Medline Plus, www.nlm.nih.gov/medlineplus/healthstatistics.html, provides numeric information on a range of health topics, including access to citations for published items through the MEDLINE/PubMed database, http://pubmed.gov.

We can further expand our exploration of health-related numeric information to a global level. One of the best-known sources of worldwide health statistics is the United Nations' World Health Organization (WHO), which makes health-related data, statistics, and publications available through a variety of forums, such as the World Health Organization Statistical Information System (WHOSIS) at www.who.int/whosis/en, the WHO Global InfoBase at www.who.int/infobase/report.aspx, and Global Health Atlas at www.who.int/globalatlas. The PanAmerican Health Organization, www.paho.org, a regional office of the WHO and part of the United Nations, focuses on health information, including numeric information, in North and South America. The United Nations' Statistics Division, http://unstats.un.org/unsd/default.htm, also provides numeric information on a variety of subjects, including health.

Numeric Information in Private Enterprises

Remember that private enterprises also contribute to the wealth of numeric information published on an ongoing basis. Businesses produce sales and expense-related information regularly for monthly, quarterly, and annual reports. In addition, they gather numeric data to monitor other aspects of company functioning, such as production and human and physical resources employed. For example, the American government requires public companies to make public disclosure of their financial information by formally registering this information with the U.S. Securities and Exchange Commission (SEC). The SEC, in turn, provides public access to SEC filings through their EDGAR database. Investors use this information to inform their stock market participation.

Businesses also produce and maintain information for public consumption on their own initiative. Most businesses provide this information via their corporate website, including numeric information about the company's financial health and consumer information. For example, Unilever, www.unilever.com, provides numeric information surrounding trading of companies it owns, as well as specialized case studies and organizational reports on such topics as sustainable development. When examining information provided on any company website, remember to consider the purpose behind making this information available to you, as well as reliability issues associated with the gathering and presentation of numeric information. Always read critically, and ask yourself not only what and how numeric information has been made available to you but also what may have been omitted.

Adding Our Own Input to the Numbers

We may also participate in the generation of numeric information ourselves. For instance, an online currency converter provides not only access to information about currency exchange rates on a given date but also enables us to calculate currency exchange for amounts of money we specify. Well-known Internet currency converters that draw on numeric information from central banks and financial services include XE Universal Currency Converter, www.xe.com/ucc, and the Financial Times' Currencies, http://markets.ft.com/ft/markets/currencies.asp.

These sites offer additional services that further facilitate our understanding of numeric information. For example, XE Universal Currency Converter offers helpful information about banking. Have you ever tried to understand the International Bank Account Number (IBAN) coding used in such transactions as a bank transfer?

Like dreams, statistics are a form of wish fulfillment.

—Jean Baudrillard (1929–)

IBAN codes are specific by country; if we take Turkey, a sample dummy IBAN code might read TR33 0006 1005 1978 6457 8413 26. XE dissects the IBAN code into its constituent parts and explains the meaning of each. In this case, TR stands for Turkey, 33 for IBAN check digits, 00061 for the specific bank's code and transit number, 00 for a reserved field, and 519786457841326 for a bank account number. Try finding IBAN coding in your country at www.xe.com/idt/.

Quick Tips Summary:
Finding Numeric Information

- Think about who publishes the type of information of interest.
- Remember that umbrella resources cover a range of topics.
- Consider whether numeric information is country or subject specific.
- Remember that numeric data and information are often available via the Internet.

Sites such as Financial Times' www.FT.com further include the latest stock market news reports, graphical depictions of currency performance, charts of currency rate projections, as well as figures for rising and falling stock prices. The Financial Times' website, in particular, offers a wealth of numeric information that can be viewed onscreen or downloaded and incorporated into a market analysis of your own, or used to track a company's financial progress on its own or comparatively against other companies. The range of numeric information provided enables us to choose whether to select from what is provided or to repackage data ourselves.

Hints for Reading and Interpreting Numeric Information

Numeric information is often reported in connection with news stories and advertisements, but what do all the numbers mean? Often, we avoid sources containing numeric information because we perceive they will be difficult to access and interpret simply on the basis that the information is numeric. When you encounter numeric information, try this approach.

First, read numeric information carefully. Decide what you actually have now and whether you have found sufficient or appropriate information to answer a query. You may find numbers that are incomplete or require repackaging to produce a full answer to a query. For example, if you wanted to locate hockey legend Maurice Richard's total goals scored during his career, you could access his game statistics at www.nhl.com. You will find Richard's profile, complete with a series of game statistics for his hockey-playing career. Once you have explored the site to establish the meaning of the various codes denoting goals (G), assists (A), games played (GP), and so on, you can note Richard's career total of 544 goals scored during regular seasons, displayed at the bottom of a table of Richard's game statistics for regular hockey seasons between 1937 and 1960. However, take care to note as well goals scored during playoff seasons, which total eighty-two. In order to provide the correct answer to your query, you need to add goal totals for both regular and playoff seasons to find that Richard actually scored 626 goals during his career, including time as a member on a number of teams. In this instance, you must combine numbers to determine an answer to your question. Suppose you wanted to find his total goals scored only while he played for the Montreal Canadiens; you would then need to tally individual totals for annual seasons for both regular and playoff seasons with this team.

There are three kinds of lies: lies, damned lies, and statistics.

—Benjamin Disraeli (1804–1881)

Large amounts of raw data may present further challenges, particularly if unorganized. Try summarizing this data. What patterns can you identify? Examining the numbers at this level will help you interpret the data you have found. For some people, this may mean constructing a

Blogspot: Interpreting World Cup Football Statistics

Germany hosted the final game of the 2006 International Federation of Association Football (FIFA) World Cup. Statistics for players are available at the official FIFA website, www.fifa.com/worldcup/archive/germany2006/statistics/players/topgoals.html. The top-scoring players' statistics are shown in table 8.1.

Visit the URL noted above and determine what each column of numeric information represents. Which player had the most penalty minutes? Who had the most shots on goal?

Writing in your blog, discuss the usefulness of a tabular presentation of numeric information for sports.

Table 8.1. Top-scoring Players' Statistics for FIFA World Cup Competition in 2006

Ctry	Player	GF	PEN	ASS	MinP	MP	SOG	SW	S	OFF	FKR	CK	W	D	L
GER	Miroslav KLOSE	5	0	1	587	7	12	8	20	5	0	0	5	1	1
ARG	Hernan CRESPO	3	0	1	308	4	5	2	7	6	0	0	3	1	0
BRA	RONALDO	3	0	1	411	5	8	7	15	10	0	0	4	0	1
FRA	Zinedine ZIDANE	3	2	1	559	6	4	5	9	1	1	19	3	3	0
ESP	David VILLA	3	2	0	210	4	7	1	8	1	2	0	3	0	1
ESP	Fernando TORRES	3	1	0	290	4	4	9	13	0	0	0	3	0	1
ARG	Maxi RODRIGUEZ	3	0	0	495	5	5	5	10	2	0	3	3	2	0
GER	Lukas PODOLSKI	3	0	0	636	7	11	12	23	8	4	4	5	1	1
FRA	Thierry HENRY	3	0	0	636	7	13	3	16	18	0	0	4	3	0

Source: International Federation of Association Football (FIFA), www.fifa.com/worldcup/archive/germany/2006/statistics/players/topgoals.html

description of numeric data; depending on the nature of your inquiry, you may need to conduct statistical analyses to consider the meaning of this data further.

In all cases, remember to read thoroughly all instructions accompanying numeric information. This includes all notes pertaining to specific elements of the information; although notes may seem trivial, they provide important clues to means of data collection and/or analyses and limitations of a particular numeric element. This information, in turn, can help you clarify what precisely you have in front of you and how you might utilize this numeric information.

Evaluating Numeric Information

Finding and interpreting numeric information enables us to recognize that we have something of potential informational value to us. Depending on the presentation of numeric information, it can be tempting to accept it. However, once we have located numeric information, we must consider its veracity and relevance to our question.

Suppose we have found a statistic that four out of five cooks prefer to use butter over margarine in their recipes. How was this claim established? Were only five cooks consulted? What does this numeric information really tell us? It is essential that we evaluate numeric information critically, just as we would other forms of information. This step is particularly important when we wish to adopt numeric information in support of arguments in our writing and even during our discussions with others.

Presenting Numeric Information

Presenting numeric information clearly is essential for good report writing. Both tables and graphs are often used to gather and make sense of numeric information. In our blog example of World Cup Football statistics, numbers were assembled by category, such as numbers of goals, penalties, and so on. You can similarly aggregate numeric information for your reports.

When deciding upon the most effective means of offering numeric information in a report, consider that your primary goal is successful communication to your audience. The numeric information you present

Quick Tips Summary:
Reading, Interpreting, Evaluating, and Presenting Numeric Information

- Read all instructions carefully.
- Identify the numeric information presented.
- Consider who produced the numeric information. Is this producer reliable?
- Evaluate the process for gathering or compiling numeric data.
- Differentiate between the date of collection or compilation of data and the publication of a statistical report.
- Read the numbers carefully.
- Be prepared to repackage the numbers provided.
- Evaluate statistical claims critically. Are claims logical and supported by the numeric information presented? What does the numeric information provided really reveal about a situation?
- Double-check numeric information to verify data and sources.
- Present numeric information clearly, using tables and graphics as appropriate to gather and organize data.

should be clear, categorized appropriately, accurate, pertinent to your argument, and referenced. Although these objectives can be achieved through a simple table in Word, graphical representation of numeric information, such as pie or bar charts using Excel, can add additional color to your report. Remember that a picture can be worth a thousand words.

He uses statistics as a drunken man uses lamp-posts—for support rather than illumination.

—Andrew Lang
(1844–1912)

Exercise: Numeric Information Hunt

1. The packaging on a ready-meal lasagna lists grams of sodium in this product as well as %DV. What does %DV mean? How are

grams of sodium related to a single serving of lasagna? What government agency explains this terminology?

2. What is a unit of alcohol? Can you locate a unit calculator on the Internet?

3. How long is the United Nations' project Water for Life scheduled to run? What statistics on availability of clean drinking water are provided by the United Nations?

4. What time is it in New York when it is 8 p.m. in Oman?

5. FreeBMD, www.freebmd.org/uk, is a U.K.-based project that provides online access to birth, death, and marriage indexes in England and Wales, 1837–1983.

   a) How many marriages registered in 1965 are currently recorded in the FreeBMD database?

   b) How is a unique record defined?

   c) What percentage of births registered in 1922 are now recorded in the FreeBMD database? Why are there four bars in each year's graph?

   d) How are percentages calculated?

   e) What potential limitations to accuracy and coverage of records are explained at the FreeBMD website?

   f) Who publishes this information?

6. What government body produces information about vital statistics in the United States? Can you locate a table of expected life expectancy published by this organization?

7. Who won the 2006 Football World Cup? What were the game statistics for the team from Costa Rica in this competition?

8. Find an online automatic weight measure converter, and convert 288 grams to pounds. Can you find a conversion table to make the same calculation?

9. What estimated amount of food is wasted in your area on an annual basis?

10. What percentage of the moon is visible when it is in the waxing crescent phase? What is the current moon phase?

CHAPTER 9

Putting Our Information Skills to Use

Our exploration of information in this book has focused on the many facets of finding information in various structures of information. We also want to be able to understand our micro information events in a wider information context. This examination of the bigger picture allows us to select a pathway through information to link smaller information events to complete a larger information puzzle we may be trying to solve.

Along the way, we often encounter barriers to resolving information problems that may make a wider information situation feel insurmountable. Rather than being stopped by possible dead ends in our acquisition and use of information, we may need to think of creative solutions to solving information problems. Sometimes the answers we need or wish to find lie in not only locating and using information but also in creating and managing information.

What You Will Learn in This Chapter

In this chapter, we learn to do the following:

- Use micro information events to help resolve macro information situations
- Think "outside the box" to overcome barriers to information
- Effectively utilize participatory web facilities and user-generated content to expand sources of potential information
- Integrate creating, managing, and sharing information into our problem solving

From Micro to Macro Information Problem Solving

Now that you have some practice with solving information problems, it is important to consider how resolving smaller information problems can lead to solving wider information problems. Genealogists offer an example of information seekers who use micro information problem solving to piece together their macro information problem, their family trees. (Note that for the purposes of this illustration, the terms *genealogy* and *family history* will be used interchangeably.) Genealogists follow steps that we can too: Assess the problem and what is needed to solve the problem, identify challenges, consider available sources of information, conduct our information search, and evaluate outcomes. A search for one's family history typically brings together many of the various types of resources we have discussed in this textbook, ranging from information published by government to information we create ourselves.

To illustrate, let's walk through the example of finding an Irish ancestor. A genealogist searching for an Irish ancestor might wish to find names of relatives, as well as information that helps portray a complete picture of that person's life, including family members, life achievements, and community involvement. Because of historical circumstances and events such as the famine, large numbers of Irish people emigrated to other countries. As a result, it is very common for many of us around the world to trace our ancestry to Ireland. Unfortunately, the nature and history of records in Ireland can make a search for one's ancestry quite a challenge. However, Irish genealogy affords us an opportunity to consider pathways around what may appear to be dead ends.

Challenges to Consider

The historical record in Ireland has been shaped by daily life circumstances. Many people can only date their family history to the nineteenth century before finding a dark period in information. Why? While some families, namely those with land, money, and titles, are often well documented in family pedigrees and local histories, more of us are hoping to locate average citizens. During the late eighteenth and early-to-middle nineteenth centuries, much of the Irish population lived as small tenant farmers or laborers. Many left during the notorious famines. We have a challenge here, because records can be fragmented, nonexistent, destroyed, or never collected. For example, births and marriages in Ireland were generally not officially recorded by the state until 1864. In addition, these records were often not kept by the Catholic Church until after 1800, and not all of these records have survived.

Where information was collected, sources disappeared for a variety of reasons. One of the major events causing loss of records was the June 1922 fire in the Four Courts, in which valuable census records, wills, and other public records were burned during the Irish Civil War. Genealogists, particularly those who are relatively new to Irish records, still refer to the fire as a problematic stumbling block in their research, even as a factor that permanently closes a door to further information finding. Substitute sources for lost information become critical in this case to overcome the perpetuated myth that "no records exist."

> A search is a search, even if it happens to disclose nothing but the bottom of a turntable.
>
> —Antonin Scalia,
> U.S. Supreme Court, 1987

The other problem that genealogists face is the scattering of records. Irish records are held in part and whole in multiple organizations and places, meaning that a wise strategy must allow for searching in multiple places and information systems.

Brainstorming Our Approach, Including Sources of Information

Typically, we would begin our search as we would any genealogical search, by consulting with family and contemporaries of our ancestors for any and all information about our ancestor, including names, dates of family events (births, deaths, marriages, and so forth), family stories, and photographs. From this point, we need to consider sources of information that might facilitate our search, and, indeed, sources that will confirm family memories. Although an Internet search is a common strategy for finding genealogical information, remember that mistakes and assumptions are often made and perpetuated online. Your skills in evaluating information and resources are critical to sifting through resources to find quality information, especially given the complexity of piecing together the puzzle of a family history.

As you begin strategizing, keep in mind the variety of information tools we have explored throughout this text. A typical starting point is Grenham's *Tracing Your Irish Ancestors*, an example of the handbooks noted in our earlier work in this book, providing titles and locations of information, as well as general advice about how to research your family tree. Remember, handbooks will help you understand organization of information in a subject area. Institutions with repositories of relevant records might logically include the National Library of Ireland, the National Archives of Ireland, the General Register Office of Ireland, the Public Records Office of

> When you go in search of honey, you must expect to be stung by bees.
>
> —Kenneth Kaunda (1924–), Zambian politician and president, *Observer*, 1983

Northern Ireland, and similar offices. In addition, we might make a list of private collections, church bodies, and library and local history collections to further our exploration. Many institutions provide information about their collections and the organization of materials, and sometimes direct digital access to collections online.

As per our earlier discussion of factual resources, several sources of this type may facilitate our work. For example, we can explore place names using such tools as *Irish Names of Places* (1893). Likewise, dictionaries of surnames offer clues about the transformation of names over time. Important sources for understanding the organization of land include the *Alphabetical Index to the Towns & Townlands of Ireland* (1877) and the *General Alphabetical Index to the Townlands and Towns, Parishes, and Baronies of Ireland* (1984).

Directories and dictionaries may also help us with spellings and occurrences of particular surnames in a given area. For example, current telephone directories lead to living holders of particular surnames. Directories published when our ancestor lived, including the *Commercial Directory of Ireland* (1820) or the *City of Dublin and Hibernian Provincial Directory* (1824), provide a retrospective snapshot of communities.

Overcoming Information Gaps and Barriers

Overcoming the challenges we have already noted, including missing and lost documentary records, requires us to think creatively. We can maximize our location of information by remembering some of our earlier discussions about how information is organized. For instance, consider who collected information, why information was kept, and how information was kept.

In the case of genealogy, understanding the collection, organization, and storage of information is critical to weaving a picture of your family history. For instance, one of the most common generators of life information is government. Think about the types of information government collects about us. In addition, consider which level of government (e.g., federal, local, or county) gathers this information. What content is made publically available and how is this information made accessible?

> *The quest for certainty blocks the search for meaning. Uncertainty is the very condition to impel man to unfold his powers.*
>
> —Erich Fromm (1900–1980), U.S. psychologist, *Man for Himself*, 1947

Successfully navigating genealogical information necessitates understanding the structure and functioning of the government bodies in question, similar to our previous exploration of information published by government.

Keep in mind the purposes for collecting information. For instance, governments seek information about their citizens for establishing taxes, as well as developing public and community services. Regular census taking offers one means of gathering information relevant to these official functions. A census can offer a wealth of information about an individual and the household in which he or she lived. As a result, the gap in Irish census records poses a significant challenge to genealogists. However, it must be remembered that not all census records were lost in the Four Courts fire of 1922. In addition, a variety of census substitutes exist that can help overcome this obstacle to finding information. Major resources that have become central as census substitutes for records lost in the Four Courts fire include *Griffith's Valuation*, 1848–1864, and *Tithe Applotment Books*, 1824–1838, both of which provide information about occupiers of land, as well as valuation of land prior to the Great Famine.

Governing bodies have also long collected information relevant to taxation purposes in Ireland. Records, such as the subsidy rolls of the 1660s that targeted nobility, clergy, and laity with the financial resources to pay taxes, poll tax returns from the same era, and hearth money rolls that compiled hearth numbers in the 1660s, were collected to support taxation. Original hearth money rolls were destroyed in the Four Courts fire; however, the Presbyterian Historical Society of Ireland had preserved copies. Remember that while information held in one location may be lost, copies held at another location can also fill an information gap.

Alternative records also exist where information about life events has been lost. For instance, the loss of original, nineteenth-century Irish wills in the Four Courts fire does not mean that all information about wills has been destroyed. First, not all wills were destroyed in the fire. Second, abstracts of wills still exist, which contain valuable family information. Indexes to wills also exist. Similarly, while original marriage license bonds burned in 1922, indexes remain available that list basic information: names of bride and groom, and date of the bond. Remember that testamentary records of births, deaths, and marriages, once collected by religious bodies, are now collected by government. Again, understanding who collected information and how the information is organized will guide your search for this information.

Blogspot: Using Ship and Passenger Information to Find People

How can travel records facilitate your search for your ancestors?

Using Ellis Island's database, www.ellisisland.org, find Annie Moore, the first passenger to arrive at Ellis Island when it opened on January 1, 1892.

Where did Annie come from? Can you locate the ship that brought her to New York on the Ellis Island website, including the ship's manifest?

How might you discover more about Annie Moore's story? Hint: Consider resources such as newspapers. Remember to evaluate the resources and information you find carefully.

What value do travel resources hold for a search for information about ancestors?

Write about your experience with travel resources in your blog.

Combining Sources of Information

Remember that consulting multiple sources in connection with your query is essential to developing a full answer for a complex information problem, such as your family history. This strategy will enable you to examine your information problem from different angles and to verify information you locate.

With our genealogy example, learning about the organization of land in an area can bring together many sources, including registers of land deeds, landed estate records, maps, ordinance surveys, and similar documents. To gather information about daily life events, we could explore records from schools, hospitals, charities, courts, military, passenger lists, and more.

Because our ancestors may have moved outside Ireland, our search may also require us to incorporate international resources into our search. Our understanding of the types of information commonly needed in genealogical research will help us, as will our understanding of how information is organized. Remember, for example, that records for births, deaths, and marriages are a commonly kept government or church record. The details collected in

Blogspot: Combining Old and New Sources of Information to Build a Family History

New and old sources can prove informative. For example, you might enlist both current and historical geographic sources to understand the physical location where your ancestor lived.

Although many things might have changed about an old street, many things may also remain the same. For instance, suppose you wanted to know more about possible ancestors who were imprisoned in the infamous French prison, the Bastille Saint-Antoine. Several famous persons, including the Man in the Iron Mask and Voltaire, spent time in the Bastille. To add to your knowledge of the lives of these individuals found in encyclopedias and biographical sources, you might wish to see the former location of the prison, Place de la Bastille, on Rue Saint-Antoine in Paris.

Using Google Street View, take a tour of Place de la Bastille. Then locate a historical map from the era of the Bastille and compare the location past and present. Write in your blog about the changes you find. What occupies the space where the Bastille once stood?

these records may differ slightly, but the basic information about an event is generally the same. In addition, these records are often indexed. Our knowledge of indexes will enable us to use these sources effectively.

There are also unique international resources that we can use to enhance our search. For instance, Library and Archives Canada, www.collec tionscanada.gc.ca, provides a searchable database of names of immigrants quarantined on Grosse-Île from 1832 to 1937. Australia's Public Records Office in Victoria, www.prov.vic.gov.au/default.asp, holds a range of information, from telegrams to police reports, about the infamous Ned Kelly gang. By combining resources, we can add to the information we have gathered about our ancestors, using the unique items we find to add interest to the family picture we build.

Creating, Managing, and Sharing Information

Once we have found information to solve one or many information problems, we should consider what we will then do with this information. Different options are open to us. We might decide to organize our information for easy retrieval by traditional means, such as indexing. However, we might also consider personalized means of adding order to the mass of information we may have accumulated, for example, Jones' (2007) personal information management system.

Again, our case of genealogy is helpful in considering our options; as avid information seekers, genealogists are often proactive in creating, managing, and sharing information. The act of assembling information for a family tree creates a new package of information. Adding life-event information, family stories, and relationships to a list of names increases the value of this information outcome. However, what genealogists then decide to do with their research is most informative for us.

Family research can produces hundreds and even thousands of names of related individuals. This information may be creatively assembled in a variety of final products, ranging from imaginative personal scrapbooking projects to more complex and original configurations of information, such as published local histories and websites devoted to a particular family grouping. Geneaologists often devise their own means and shared means of organizing and disseminating information.

Not only does the Internet figure prominently in genealogical research but it is also central to the creation, management, and sharing of this type of information. As a result, tools such as e-mail, discussion lists, and websites enable finding information, as well as sharing and collaborating on research. The Internet has facilitated collaboration and sharing of information between individuals and groups around the world. User-generated content offers an opportunity to share with each other and collectively gather, assess, and manage information. As Web 2.0 facilities have become available, genealogical researchers have begun to adopt them. For example, some genealogists are blogging. In recognition of this growing use of blogs, *Cyndi's List of Genealogy Sites on the Internet* now provides a link to a specialized Genealogy Blog Finder, http://blogfinder.genealogue.com. Institutions also support this development with their adoption of recent Internet services, such as Flickr and YouTube, used to provide public access to such information as virtual exhibitions.

This growth of tools and resources continues to facilitate our access to and use of information. As we have seen with our example of genealogical research, not only can we overcome obstacles to finding information, we can also be imaginative in how we create, manage, and share the information we have found. Now, what will you do with the information you find?

Exercise

1. Devise a strategy to establish your family tree in Ireland.
   a. What sorts of resources would inform your search? Why?
   b. What resource would you use first?
   c. What obstacles might hinder your search?
2. One of your ancestors immigrated to the United States during the Irish famine. How might you locate that individual? How might you find that person's descendants?
3. One of your ancestors married in England. How could you locate the marriage record for that couple?
   a. What information would you need to conduct this search?
   b. How is information about marriage recorded and organized?

4. Using free wiki software, such as FlexWiki, http://sourceforge
   .net/projects/flexwiki, and working in a group, research the
   life history of Horatio Nelson. What sort of information can
   you bring together in your wiki? How would you present this
   information?

CHAPTER 10

Maintaining Information Literacy Levels in a Changing World

At this point, you should be familiar with many of the basics of finding information. You might consider this a good time to stop and rest—after all, you've nearly covered the whole of this book and you have learned some valuable new approaches to locating information in your academic and daily lives. However, it is important to remember that you are really only embarking on a lifelong path of learning. The International Federation of Library Associations and Institutions (IFLA) (Garner 2006) identified information literacy as a critical part of social and economic development, empowering us to function as citizens and enhancing our quality of life. Maintaining and building on your current level of information literacy is essential to keeping up the skills you may wish to draw upon at any time in your life.

What You Will Learn in This Chapter

In this chapter, we consider what we have learned and explore means of retaining and continuing our understanding of the varied and evolving world of information around us. You will learn to do the following:

- Review reasons for learning continuously
- Implement positive practices for maintaining fluency with information

Why Adopt a Continuous Learning Approach?

Continuous learning acknowledges that we learn over time. It is important to allow ourselves time to absorb and reinforce skills as we learn them.

Adopting a continuous or ongoing learning approach has several advantages:

- *Learning continuously means that we are constantly taking in and evaluating new information.* Learning continuously means that as new information and resources appear, we can apply our analytical skills to understanding, evaluating, and using these new items. This enables us to absorb information as we go along, invoking this process of analysis as we proceed. As we repeat this process, we reinforce efficient patterns of information behavior we have adopted, while remaining open to new, potentially more effective means of locating information.

  > Anyone who stops learning is old, whether at twenty or eighty. Anyone who keeps learning stays young.
  >
  > —Henry Ford

- *Learning helps to maintain an active mind.* Never mind the saying, "You can't teach an old dog new tricks." Learning is something we can and should do throughout our lives. The act of learning can give us purpose, help us remain mentally agile, and make us feel younger.
- *Learning helps us cope with change.* One thing we can count on is constant change. That change can be rapid and/or dramatic. For example, tools we use to locate information, such as computer systems, can change multiple times and without warning. Some resources change entirely in organization with every updated version. However, with continuous learning, you are no longer learning to use a particular tool and considering your learning complete. Now that you have taken a problem-solving approach, you are capable of accomplishing more than learning about a particular tool. You can apply this process to any situation and quickly adapt to a new tool, new resource, or new circumstance. Use continuous learning and the problem-solving approach to embrace change.
- *Learning on an ongoing basis means that we have information and skills at our fingertips when we need them.* Through continuous learning, we can remain current with new developments. The result is that we can say good-bye to crisis management. We are prepared or in a situation where

we can prepare ourselves to manage and deal effectively with change. We are ready to meet challenges on an ongoing basis.

General Tips for Maintaining Information Literacy

There is no magic wand for maintaining information literacy. Rather, now that you have learned about a problem-solving process and have applied it to some information problems, you must continue the learning process. Understanding the process of locating, evaluating, and using information provides a useful foundation for further information seeking. As you continue, you should also remain open to learning new or advanced methods of accessing and analyzing information.

A few guidelines will help you maintain the level of information literacy you have achieved, as well as improve upon your skills.

> *A good head and good heart are always a formidable combination. But when you add to that a literate tongue or pen, then you have something very special.*
>
> —Nelson Mandela

Remember learning is a process. Focus on the process of problem solving. This will help you concentrate on building a strategy to overcome an information challenge. Try not to be derailed by the apparent newness of an information query or uncertainty about potentially available sources. Remember that by adopting a problem-solving process, you are freed from thinking in terms of sources and you can focus on building a strategic approach for any situation. Learning is a process that can empower you.

It all takes time. Allow yourself the time you require to work your way through the problem-solving process each time you approach an information problem, including allowing yourself time to go through each part of the process. Over time, you will become more familiar with the process and pathways to information and you will improve your ability to locate and deal with information more efficiently.

Remember what you learn as you learn. Remembering what you learn is critical to applying new knowledge to new situations. Practice these key guidelines for remembering what you learn:

- *Understand what you are learning.* If you cannot understand part or all of what you are attempting to learn, you will not retain that information for future use. It is essential to comprehend the task you are performing and to understand why you need to perform that task, so that you better understand what it is you are trying to achieve. Memorizing without understanding will not enable you to apply knowledge to another situation.

- *Repeat things you learn.* This entails more than memorization. You want to review material that you learn to keep it present in your memory. Remember, becoming information literate is not a one-time activity. This is a life-changing commitment.
- *Give learning your full attention.* To focus completely, you need to be alert, rested, and ready to devote your time to the task at hand.
- *Make the information meaningful to you.* We remember things closer to us better than information that has no apparent relevance to our lives.

Practice makes perfect. Once you have successfully completed the process of solving an information problem, you should feel confident to try to solve other information problems. Remember, you have gone through the process now and you *can* do it again.

Use it or lose it! Be conscious of your information seeking and the patterns you follow on an ongoing basis. Analyze the approach you have taken in a particular situation and revisit that approach in a similar circumstance in which you require information. Keep applying the problem-solving process at all times. Continuously working at applying the process will make effective and efficient information seeking part of your natural behavioral pattern. You want to sustain your learning, not regress.

Share the experience. If you can show another person how to work logically through the steps to solving an information problem, then you have learned the process and have become comfortable with it.

Special Cases

MAINTAINING INFORMATION LITERACY IN AN ACADEMIC SETTING

In an academic environment, there is even more pressure on you to learn and retain that learning. Future career prospects can depend upon high scholastic achievement. It is essential that you keep up with the pace of academic practice to ensure ongoing success with your studies and future endeavors. Although you may feel overwhelmed by times with the amount of work that your courses demand of you, you can prepare to meet the challenges of formal education.

DEVELOP AND PRACTICE GOOD STUDY HABITS

Regardless of where you are now in the educational process, stop now and take stock. Where are you? What have you achieved so far? Now consider your goals as you continue your education. Good study habits can help you achieve these goals.

Developing effective study habits involves ongoing commitment and lots of hard work. You will take from your education what you put into it. Your instructors will help guide you, but at the end of the day, the responsibility for grappling with a given subject is yours. Get started now by preparing yourself for study with effective study skills. Try incorporating the following ideas into your study patterns.

First, attend your lectures. Students often undervalue the importance of investing in this aspect of their education. Your presence in the classroom ensures that you know what material has been discussed. Your lecturers are subject experts. Listen actively to what they have to tell you. Engage in discussion and critical evaluation of the subject matter. Ask probing questions. Take notes that accurately represent the content of your lectures, including the material covered in class discussions. Note taking is a special skill through which you learn to identify the significant points from a lecture. Do not depend upon lecture handouts that are distributed. Your notes will help you improve your recall of lecture content, assist you with course assessment, and may become a resource for future reference in your work and daily life.

As you prepare to study, start by creating a positive environment in which you can concentrate. For some students, the most conducive environment for studying is a quiet library reading room. For others, a favorite study environment is a desk in a dormitory room. Whatever environment you select, be sure that you will have few distractions. You need to be able to focus on the material you need to review.

Start studying at the beginning of the semester, when your formal classes begin. If you study as you learn, you will understand and retain more material. Set aside regular times for studying. Commit yourself to

Quick Tips Summary: Study Smart!

How effective are your study habits? Here is a checklist of tips to help you improve your study skills and study smart!

- Attend your lectures.
- Take notes that accurately represent the content of your lectures.
- Create a positive environment for studying.
- Start studying at the beginning of the semester.
- Set aside regular times for studying.
- Review lessons after each lecture.
- Review periodically as well, for example, at the end of every week. Studying is cumulative.
- Study in groups as well as on your own.
- Be your own teacher.

these times; mark them on your calendar for the coming weeks and stick to this schedule. You should review your individual lessons immediately after each lecture, as well as cumulatively on a periodic basis. For example, you might plan to review the week's lectures at the end of each week.

Although there may be times when you prefer to study alone, set aside time to work with others as well. Organize a study group and meet regularly to work together to discuss and brainstorm approaches to understanding theoretical concepts or to solving particular types of problems (e.g., mathematics equations). The input of another person might help you see a problem from a different perspective.

Be your own teacher. Read and reread the assigned readings, making notes about the content and significance of the points made in these readings as you read. Explore new ideas fully, seeking out additional information to supplement areas with which you may not be familiar.

Often the hardest part of studying is getting started. Once you get started and establish a regular routine for yourself, you will find that you are able to carry on studying with greater ease.

EXCEL AT ASSESSMENT

Once you have your timetable and submission dates for assignments, plan your time for the semester to facilitate completion of all tasks in time.

Record all assignment due dates and examination dates on your calendar. For example, you can enter items into calendar software, such as Google Calendar, www.google.com/calendar, or Outlook. Then, by synchronizing your calendar with the calendar in your mobile phone, Netbook computer, or other device, you can easily access your calendar at all times. Now, count backward in your calendar from each of these dates and reserve a generous amount of time to complete each assignment or prepare for each examination.

Begin your assignments as soon as you receive your assignment instructions. You should plan your time to accommodate analyzing the assignment requirements, locating information in appropriate resources in support of your work, and preparing a report for submission. Do not try to complete all of these steps at the last minute. Remember that you have been given your assignments for a reason; explore the assignment fully and give yourself the opportunity to learn from this exercise.

Start preparing for midterm tests and final examinations at the beginning of your course. Locate copies of past examinations for your course as soon as possible. Implement a study plan early. Consider the various types of examination questions, such as multiple choice, short essay, and full essay, and plan accordingly for your examination. Start now to prepare for definitional questions, writing terms and meanings on opposite sides of note cards and quizzing yourself when you have spare time. The ride home on the bus is an excellent time to practice! It is essential to allow yourself

Quick Tips Summary: Planning for Assignments and Examinations

- Plan your time at the beginning of the semester. Mark important dates on your calendar, such as submission dates for assignments, project due dates, and examination dates.
- Reserve appropriate time to complete each assignment by the submission date.
- Begin assignments as soon as you receive them.
- Begin studying for examinations at the beginning of your course.
- Obtain copies of past examinations for a course at the beginning of the semester.
- Allow sufficient time to prepare for the tasks you must complete.

Blogspot: Evaluating Our Improving Information Literacy

How have your information literacy skills changed since you began reading this textbook? Write in your blog, describing your information world at this time.

Locate your earlier blog entry in which you described your information world. Compare your perspectives then and now.

What new goals will you set now to continue to develop your information literacy?

the time you need to absorb the material covered in a course. An examination is not intended to be a test of the information you can memorize at the last minute; rather, an examination is meant to verify that you have learned a set of materials over the duration of a course. Give yourself the opportunity to prepare sufficiently to excel at this task.

In the examination hall, remember to plan carefully the time allotted for the examination. Read the examination instructions. Select the questions you will answer, if you are given a choice of a series of questions. Take time to plan, in point form, your responses to each question you will answer. This entire process will take a very short time at the beginning of the exam, but it will reduce possible panic reactions and will help keep you focused and progressing smoothly through the exam paper.

MANAGE YOUR TIME FOR SUCCESS

A significant factor in your achievement in your studies is time management. Success with many of the tips we have discussed in this chapter depends upon your ability to plan your time. Managing your time effectively will enable you sufficient time to analyze critically the information you have found and to apply it to tasks, such as essays, presentations, and examinations.

The Future Is Now

Learning is an ongoing process. Even when we have mastered a particular skill or have understood a concept, there may be more we can learn. Even accessing information is not an end in itself. We need to assess that information in the context of our information problem. There is no time like the present to develop and maintain an understanding of the information world around us. Remember that you are investing your time in your future and that future begins now.

To make the most of your developing problem-solving skills, try to apply what you have learned in different areas of your life at all times. Think about what you are doing as you search for information, continuously reviewing your information-seeking strategy as well as the progress of your search. In addition, integrate constant evaluation of information into this process and be aware of the decisions you are making as you move forward. Remaining vigilant about the means by which you approach information problems will help you maintain the level of information literacy you have attained.

Exercise

Using Google Calendar, Outlook, or your mobile phone calendar, create a study calendar and plan your pathway through a formal course or self-directed learning program.

Blogspot: Evaluating Our Planning Skills

Follow your calendar study plan for two weeks, writing about your progress in your blog. Now it is time to evaluate your study plan. Reflect on your blog entries and answer the following questions:

- How well have you adhered to your study plan?
- How have you used your calendar, for example, to document events or to set event reminders?
- How has your plan facilitated your learning goals?

CHAPTER 11

It's a Wrap! Some Final Thoughts on Finding and Using Information

Successful Information Seeking

Knowledge is happiness, because to have knowledge—broad, deep knowledge—is to know true ends from false, and lofty things from low. To know the thoughts and deeds that have marked man's progress is to feel the great heart-throbs of humanity through the centuries; and if one does not feel in these pulsations a heavenward striving, one must indeed be deaf to the harmonies of life.

—Helen Keller (1880–1968),
The Story of My Life, part 1,
chapter 20, 1903

At this moment, you have, hopefully, now experienced at least one successful information search following the advice in this book. You may have located a new piece of information that led to the next step in your quest for information or provided closure to your information query. Success in the process of identifying, locating, and evaluating information can mean different things to different information seekers. It's essential to pause and reflect on our journey through information. Remember the primary goal of your information search. Have you located appropriate, reliable information that satisfies your objective?

When All Else Fails . . .

In spite of our best efforts, we sometimes encounter situations in which we do not locate information to satisfy the information problem we have identified. This experience can prove frustrating; however, there are some remaining tactics we can employ to resolve an information problem.

First, revisit your information search plan. Reconsider the choices you made at the beginning of your search. Recall the initial information problem and review your conceptualization of the problem and possible approaches to resolving it, including the identification of search terms, potential sources of information, and your overall search plan. What alternative approaches might help you? Revise your initial search plan and try your search again.

In addition, remember that while you are actively searching for information, a little browsing may also facilitate your search. Has there been a new development in the organization of a particular type of information that might help you revisit a current or old information problem? New information resources and tools are constantly being produced. Try to be thorough in your consideration of possible problem-solving approaches.

When all else fails, you may need to consider whether the information you wish to find actually exists. Although you may have tried a variety of approaches, it is possible that the information you wish to find has not been organized in an information system or has not been collected. If you have exhausted all possibilities, the information may not exist or

> Every experience in life enriches one's background and should teach valuable lessons.
>
> —Mary Barnett Gilson (1877–?), *What's Past Is Prologue*, chapter 24, 1940

perhaps is not in the form you need or want. Depending on your own time and resources, you may need to gather and organize information yourself in order to satisfy the information problem you need to answer.

Before you decide an answer to your information problem cannot be found, however, be certain that this is, in fact, the case. When in doubt, ask a librarian or information professional for help. They are specially trained to help you. And remember that two heads are often better than one when working on particularly challenging information problems.

Quick Tips Summary:
Strategies for Success When
Information Cannot Be Found

- Revisit your search plan.
- Consider alternative search approaches.
- Consider alternative information resources.
- Compile data or information yourself.
- Ask an information professional for assistance.

Factors Influencing Success in the Hunt for Information

Ultimately, success in your information search depends on several factors. Your understanding of your need to find information—that is, the information problem you are planning to solve—will help you decide when you are finally satisfied with your information search.

Additionally, systems of information organization and management may not always cater to your specific information needs and may be limited in their functionality. For example, remember our comparison of Google Books and OCLC's WorldCat and the quirks of each. By developing strategies to communicate as effectively as possible with a system, you can take advantage of a range of system search options available to you and improve your chances of extracting the information you require. Patience and perseverance mixed with some creativity in our approach to an information problem can help us achieve extraordinary results.

Most importantly, believe in yourself as an information seeker. If you tell yourself that you can find information, you will improve your chances of locating that information. A positive attitude will help you approach new problems confidently and will empower you to overcome obstacles that appear in the course of your search.

Some Final Advice as You Close This Book

Congratulations! You have covered a great deal of material in the course of this book. You should have an edge in the complex information world that awaits you. Most critically, you should now have developed a problem-solving approach to the process of finding, evaluating, and using information. By mastering problem-solving skills, you have equipped yourself to meet information challenges with confidence.

In addition, you should have an enhanced understanding of systems of information in different formats. Although we may wish for information systems that can understand and even anticipate our needs, the reality is that we must still negotiate information systems, whether a computerized database or a printed source, and we must be able to understand the means of organization of information adopted in each instance. The principles for organizing different types of information are valuable to consider as you approach any information resource.

> *Understanding is the wages of faith.*
>
> —St. Augustine (354–430)

You should now be prepared to tackle any information problem. No one can promise you that an information search will be easy, but you should feel confident to tackle the information problems you face every day. If you ever feel doubt, feel free to come back and review the relevant aspects of the structures of organized information and the process of finding and evaluating information outlined here anytime. This book is your guide for the future. Practice what you have learned here whenever you need or want information. Above all else, enjoy your journey through information!

Sources for
Further Exploration

Chapter 2

Association of College and Research Libraries (ACRL). 2000. *Information Literacy Competency Standards for Higher Education*. Available: www.ala.org/ala/mgrps/divs/acrl/standards/informationliteracycompetency.cfm.

————. 2000. *Information Literacy. Standards Toolkit*. Available: www.ala.org/ala/mgrps/divs/acrl/issues/infolit/standards/standardstoolkit.cfm.

Association of Colleges and Research Libraries. 2003. *Introduction to Information Literacy*. Available: www.ala.org/ala/mgrps/divs/acrl/issues/infolit/overview/intro/index.cfm, with further sources available at www.ala.org/ala/mgrps/divs/acrl/issues/infolit/index.cfm.

Bruce, C. 2003. *Seven Faces of Information Literacy: Towards Inviting Students into New Experiences*. Presentation. Available: http://crm.hct.ac.ae/events/archive/2003/speakers/bruce.pdf.

Campbell, S. 2004. *Defining Information Literacy in the 21st Century*. Paper presented at World Library and Information Congress, 70th IFLA General Conference and Council, Buenos Aires, Argentina. Available: www.ifla.org/IV/ifla70/papers/059e-Campbell.pdf.

Chartered Institute of Library and Information Professionals (CILIP). *Information Literacy*. Available: www.cilip.org.uk/get-involved/advocacy/learning/information-literacy/pages/default.aspx.

Council of Australian University Librarians (CAUL). 2001. *Information Literacy Standards*. Canberra, Australia. Available: www.caul.edu.au/caul-doc/InfoLit Standards2001.doc.

International Federation of Library Associations and Institutions (IFLA). *Information Literacy Section*. Available: www.ifla.org/VII/s42/index.htm.

Nahl, Diane. 2007. The Centrality of the Affective in Information Behavior. In D. Nahl and D. Bilal, eds., *Information and Emotion: The Emergent Affective Paradigm in Information Behavior Research and Theory* (pp. 3–37). Medford, NJ: Information Today.

Shenk, D. 1997. *Data Smog*. San Francisco: Harper.

———. 2007. The e-decade: Was I right about the dangers of the Internet in 1997? *Slate Magazine*, July 25, 1997. Available: www.slate.com/id/2171128/.

Stern, C. M. 2002. *Information Literacy "Unplugged": Teaching Information Literacy without Technology*. White Paper prepared for UNESCO, the U.S. National Commission on Libraries and Information Science, and the National Forum on Information Literacy, for use at the information literacy meeting of experts, Prague, Czech Republic.

Wilson, T. D. 1999. Models in information behavior research. *Journal of Documentation* 55(3): 249–70. Available: http://informationr.net/tdw/publ/papers/1999JDoc.html.

Chapter 3

Internet Public Library (IPL). www.ipl.org.

RefDesk.com. www.refdesk.com.

Reference.com. www.reference.com.

Tapscott, D., and A. D. Williams. 2006. *Wikinomics*. London: Atlantic Books.

Weinberger, D. 2007. *Everything Is Miscellaneous: The Power of the New Digital Disorder*. New York: Times Books.

Chapter 4

Hill, B. 2005. *Google Search and Rescue for Dummies*. Hoboken, NJ: John Wiley & Sons.

Schein, A. M. 2005. *Find It Online: The Complete Guide to Online Research*. 4th ed. Tempe, AZ: Facts on Demand Press.

Search Engine Watch. Available: http://searchenginewatch.com.

Smith, A. 2005. *Criteria for Evaluation of Internet Information Resources*. Available: www.vuw.ac.nz/staff/alastair_smith/evaln/index.htm#Authority.

Chapter 5

Libdex—Index to 18,000 Libraries. Available: www.libdex.com
Library of Congress. *Gateway to Library Catalogs.* (Worldwide catalogues). Available: www.loc.gov/z3950/gateway.html#A.
National Library Catalogues Worldwide. University of Queensland, Australia. Available: www.library.uq.edu.au/ssah/jeast.
UNESCO Libraries Portal—Library Catalogues. Available: www.unesco.org/web world/portal_bib/Reference/Catalogues.
UNESCO. *World Digital Library.* Available: www.wdl.org.

Chapter 6

Mathews, B. S. 2004. Gray Literature: Resources for Locating Unpublished Resource. *College and Research Libraries News* 65 (3). Available: www.ala.org/ala/mgrps/divs/acrl/publications/crlnews/2004/mar/graylit.cfm.

Chapter 7

King, G. 2009. *Improve Your Writing Skills.* London: Collins.
Lipson, C. 2006. *Cite Right: A Quick Guide to Citation Styles—MLA, APA, Chicago, the Sciences, Professions and More.* Chicago: Chicago University Press.
Staines, G. M., M. Bonacci, and K. Johnson. 2008. *Social Sciences Research: Research, Writing, and Presentation Strategies for Students.* 2nd ed. Lanham, MD: Scarecrow Press.

Chapter 8

Internet World Stats: Usage and Population Statistics. Available: www.internet worldstats.com.
Nation Master. Available: www.nationmaster.com.
United Nations Statistics Division. Available: http://unstats.un.org/unsd.
World Clock (pooling statistics on a variety of topics from a variety of sources). Available: www.poodwaddle.com/worldclock.swf.
World Fact Book. Available: https://www.cia.gov/library/publications/the-world-factbook/index.html.

Worldometers: World Statistics Updated in Real Time. Available: www.worldo meters.info.

Chapter 9

Cyndi's List of Genealogy Sites on the Internet. Available: www.cyndislist.com.

Grenham, J. 2006. *Tracing Your Irish Ancestors: The Complete Guide.* Baltimore, MD: Genealogical Publishing.

Jones, W. 2007. *Keeping Found Things Found.* San Francisco, CA: Morgan Kaufmann.

Chapter 10

Garner, S. D. 2006. *High-Level Colloquium on Information Literacy and Lifelong Learning: Report of a Meeting Sponsored by UNESCO, NFIL, and IFLA.* Available: www.ifla.org/III/wsis/High-Level-Colloquium.pdf.

The Information Literacy Website. Available: www.informationliteracy.org.uk.

UNESCO and IFLA. *InfoLit Global.* Available: www.infolitglobal.info.

Index

ACRL. *See* Association of Colleges and Research Libraries
affective behavior, 8, 9–10
ALA. *See* American Library Association
almanac, 21, 34, *37*
American Library Association (ALA), 13, *41*
annotation, 84, 96, 97
assessment, 127; planning, 128–30, 131; time management, 130
Association of Colleges and Research Libraries (ACRL), 13
atlas. *See* geographic resources
author, 44, 68–69, 71, 75–76. *See also* researcher
autobiography, 21
Awasu, 94

barriers to information, overcoming, 4, 14, 113, 117–18
bibliographic control, 2, 4, 58–59, 64, 68, 76–77
bibliographic reference, 58, 86
bibliographic software. *See* reference list

bibliography, 3, 19, 58, 59–60, 65, 88, 91, 95–96, 97, 102; location, 59–60; national, 59; subject, 59; trade, 59. *See also* reference list
bibliography, annotated. *See* reference list, annotated
bibliography of bibliographies, 59–60
biographical resource, 21–22, *37*, *119*
biography, 21, 32, 58
blog, 5, 14–16, 28, *49*, *52*, *64*, *70*, 74, 80, 81, *93*, *94*, *107*, 109, *118*, *119*, 121, *130*, *131*; Blogger.com, 15, *94*; blogspot, *49*, *52*, *64*, *70*, 78, *93*, *94*, *107*, *118*, *119*, *130*, *131*; creation, 15–16; location, 26–27, 121; ranking, 26
book review. *See* review
Boole, George (1815–1864), 46
Boolean, 40, 46, 47; operators, 46–49; order of operations, 48–49; parentheses, 47, 48

catalogue, 3, 19, 41, 50, 58, 59, 60–61, 63, 64, 65, 70, *72*, *73*, 81, *89*, 95, 102
Cataloguing in Publication (CIP), 69

About the Author

Crystal Fulton holds her doctorate in library and information science. She has taught information and writing skills to students at all levels, both in her native Canada and in Ireland. Currently, she is a faculty member at the School of Information and Library Studies, University College Dublin, where she teaches information finding and evaluating skills to both undergraduate and postgraduate students.